# Jesus -
# The Capernaum Stories

## From Capernaum to a Desert Oasis
## Ordinary People.
## Extraordinary Lives.

Karl C Evans

*Karl Evans*
*Oct 22, 2016*

Cover design by Karl C Evans
EAN-13:9781453657447
ISBN-10:1453657444

# Dedication

"Jesus Touched Them" is dedicated to the many communities Donella and I have served. In our fifty years together, we have served and worked with congregations across the United States in all fifty states, Canada and Mexico. We have also established friendships in many nations, including India, Indonesia, Japan, Sweden, Iran, Iraq, United Kingdom, Germany, New Zealand and others. Their questions, their logic, and their eager search for faith have shaped this book. May their quest shape your life as it has shaped mine.

Karl C Evans

# Table of Contents

# Foreword

We are privileged people. Living at the start of the 21$^{st}$ century reveals to us realities of life around the world. We can know foods and medical care, education patterns and burial practice from centuries ago and decades ahead. This can be very helpful in our own lives.

However, we find it difficult to know relationships, joys and sorrows of years ago. Even with the exquisite record keeping of the Bible, we usually fail to hold clear images of Jesus' life. We know little of his hopes and dreams, his temptations and his sense of failure. As for those around Jesus, except a few such as Paul, we know next to nothing of their personal lives.

This book offers some handles for today's readers. These handles are simply visions of the life and ministry of Jesus in today's words and expressions. The gospels record many confrontations between Jesus and those around him.

Some he touched were disciples; some were antagonists. Some were passers-by; some were violently involved in events. Many just did not care about him. Most are not named in the Gospels. Nevertheless, Jesus influenced every life he touched.

The stories of this book speak of the touch of Jesus on these lives. By seeing Jesus' touch on those lives, perhaps we can more clearly feel his touch on our own realities. We feel him touching our tears and our fears. When he gives order to our confusions, we feel stronger. It is the same whether Jesus touches us or a farmer of two thousand years ago.

A word of explanation. Each story is given a "Gospel Time:" Assume a time line for the overall Gospel story, somewhat similar to the function of Anno Domini, or A.D. The opening event for our line is "001", or just before the birth of Jesus.  The apparent first baptism after the disciples began their missionary work is "600" The final event is some time in the future.

In our line, the line runs from 000 to 600 for the Gospel time. As I write stories reflecting later events, their time line will a number code larger than 600. Additional stories from the life of Jesus will be between "000" and "600." Stories of earlier events will have negative time lines. In this manner, I can continue to write more stories for history, easily placing them in appropriate times for the reader.

These two books of Gospel stories are companions for each other.  Jesus - The Nazareth Stories is companion to and flows into Jesus - The Capernaum Stories. Scriptures noted  are provided to help build an awareness of Biblical thought as response to the ideas of the basic underlined passage. Various lectionary systems may use some of these passages. The reading dates or seasons listed are either a median of lectionary usage or my own suggestions.

Finally, I have a strong sense of my own relationship with Jesus. If I knew, without a doubt, that Jesus was an ordinary mortal man, with no powers or position different from anyone else, I would still try to follow him. I like his style, his mission, his compassion. Imitating him would still be impossible, but I like to believe I would try.

But I believe Jesus somehow has some godly portion (whatever that is) it is easier to be motivated to understand his will as my call. However, answering that call by the Christ is no easier than answering that call if spoken by some non-divine human.

So enjoy my books. If you wish the stories to be told differently, the podium is yours. If you wish to use these stories as sermons, class discussions, family discussions or personal articles, go right ahead. I have used them all in these ways. Just note where you found them. Plagiarism is sinful only if proper credit is not given.

Have fun.

Karl Evans

# 36. New Wine
## Mark 2:13-22
How to get a new start.
Pentecost     Gospel Time: 330


Philo watched the little procession moving along the shore of the Sea of Galilee just east of Capernaum. Peering out from under the shade with a mild curiosity, Philo was only curious who was walking with Levi.

Levi was a good neighbor to Philo. Levi often mixed some of Philo's daily chores with his own. Levi needed water from the community well. Philo was about out of water now. Levi often brought some extra for Philo. Philo had few other friends. After Delilah died, Philo was very lonely. He talked sometimes with his customers. Almost every day he talked with the men who gathered every morning in the shade of Levi's tent flap.

Philo and Levi each had tents in the agora. That is the Greek word for marketplace. If Levi happened to spot a tear in his own tent, he patched it. Then Levi checked Philo's tent for tears or holes. If he found something, he patched the problem. When Philo first saw Levi's work, he tried to protest. Levi simply smiled.

"Philo, old friend, you have done so much for me. Now I have unpacked my thread and needle. I have fixed my own tent, and I just notice this tiny little spot on yours. It will take me just a moment to fix it. I will never have to spend any time to make it look as good as mine."

Levi smiled at Philo. He knew that the two men were good for each other. They enjoyed being neighbors in the agora, the marketplace. Philo was the older man, but that was a problem only because he grew more frail as time passed.

Philo had a small business he ran from his tent. Philo sold several different kinds of writing material from his tent of business. He made scrolls or even just small sheets of paper from different reeds and grasses. Lamb skin, calf leather, rabbit skin, any kind of skin could be prepared with a pale finish. Then Philo could write a letter, or a deed of sale on it.

Philo prepared special quills for writing on different surfaces. The finest quills would write on linen paper for very important or official documents. Heavier and sturdier quills wrote on leather or sheets of bark.

Philo even special clay for very permanent writings. Philo bought this clay from a neighbor who brought it down from the north, along the road to Damascus. This clay was in a deposit along the Jordan River flowing from the North to the Sea of Galilee.

Any who might purchase this clay would need to wet it down. Then the writer formed it into a flat surface for writing. Then, by using a knife or a sharp stick, one could easily write or draw on the clay. Then they could fire the sheet to make it very strong.

Philo could read and write both koine Greek and classic Hebrew plus Aramaic. He learned some of his skill from the rabbis as a young boy. Much of his ability came from either watching or talking with the travelers who came to his stall. When a traveler came to him to purchase equipment, Philo often watched carefully. Each new customer looked at the quill or piece of papyrus paper. When Philo learned some new trick, he tried it out. He sometimes cut a quill feather in a different direction. Often he mixed a different berry or piece of tree bark in his ink. Someone said it was their preference. Much of his skill was self-taught.

When someone needed a letter or a document, Philo was quite willing to prepare it for them. For a price, of course. He sat on the ground next to his little table. Slowly and methodically Philo wrote whatever the customer asked.

Often, some customer brought him a letter or document to decipher. Philo liked this very much. He paid good attention to letters or official documents coming to his customers from far away. Philo found many new ideas and news of the world within those letters.

Philo had trouble with his back and his legs. Even his

eyes were beginning to go bad from years of close work. Sometimes he had to ask his friend, Levi, to read some fine document for him. Philo kept working. He could not afford to stop. His little business gave him food, shelter, clothing and friends.

Philo had another source of a small income. Once one of his friends suggested that he might add some wine skins and water skins to his product line. It really made sense. Philo always had a few skins on hand for writing purposes. Sheep, rabbit and goat skins were most popular. In Capernaum, with so many travelers, it was a pretty good market.

So Philo sometimes found a special skin of some animal that made a good water or wine container. Then he stitched it up carefully to produce a watertight container. He always tried to use leather thongs made from the same animal to tie up the skin.

Philo did not sell many wine skins or water skins. Many people made their own. Also, other men and women in Capernaum prepared the same product line for sale or trade. The steady flow of travelers through the town made a good market. They were moving along the road to Damascus or Jerusalem or Tyre or Babylon.

Levi, Philo's good friend, was a tax collector by trade. It was a much simpler life, but it did have its own troubles and dangers. No one enjoys paying taxes, but every government collects taxes. Collecting taxes makes it possible to build roads and raise armies. Collecting taxes builds palaces for the rich and prisons for the poor.

So Levi collected taxes for the nation. He collected for the regional government. Levi collected for his home city, Capernaum. Whatever manner of taxes the government said, Levi collected. Property tax. Tax on travelers passing through with their caravans. Tax on writing equipment. Whatever. If the government said "Tax!", Levi collected.

For a fee, of course. Levi simply kept some tax he collected. Sometimes one of his customers offered Levi an extra little sum if he simply ignored some taxable item. This was a means of gaining much extra wealth. Levi tried to avoid these matters. If he were caught cheating by the government, they could put him in prison, or even kill him. So he tried to stay honest in his work.

Levi's extra income came from a different set of taxes. Even the temple in Jerusalem levied taxes. Some people said King Herod's reason for rebuilding the temple in Jerusalem did not concern allowing faithful Jews to worship. The common thought was Herod expected he could get his hands on the temple taxes. He especially thought he could control the temple tax coming in from faraway lands; lands outside those he controlled. Much tax money came in from Egypt, and Libya, and Syria, and

India, and Rome. So Herod did what he could to convince the Jews to keep sending their tax money to the temple.

In the agora, the market place of Capernaum, the tents of Philo and Levi were next to each other. These friends often worked together in their little businesses. Often Levi need some official document concerning a tax or property matter. When he needed this, he turned to his friend Philo for help. When Philo need a little extra space to store some inventory overnight, he turned to Levi. If they threatened Philo, Levi came to the rescue by speaking to one of Levi's friends at the army post. The government and the temple organization took good care of the tax collectors and their friends.

Philo repaid the tax man, Levi, by being a good friend. The grumblers at the synagogue condemned Levi for collecting taxes. Philo tried to both defend Levi and pass on some words of strength. Because Philo rarely went to the synagogue, he and Levi had a common rank in society. Tax collector and sinner. Two of a kind.

Philo saw something new as he sat in the shade of Levi's tent that beautiful spring morning. The scene changed his sense of his own life. Four men walked slowly toward the tent where Philo sat on the ground. Levi walked by the side of Jesus. Jesus was carpenter who recently moved to town. In only a few days, Jesus made many friends. He picked up some good business for his trade as a carpenter. In addition, Jesus had gained some reputation as a healer and personal counselor. The other two men, local fishermen who worked the Sea of Galilee, were long-time friends. They came around often to visit Philo.

Jesus, Levi and the others settled themselves in a circle under Levi's tent awning. These were always good times. The group in front of the tax collector's tent might be just Levi and Philo. It might include the newcomer, Jesus. Occasionally the group included a dozen of the men of Capernaum. The attendance did not matter. This was a good time for every man who joined the little group. Lots of laughter and stories. Even some that they could repeat.

This group was Philo's family. When Philo's wife, Delilah, died a couple years ago, on a sabbath before Passover, Philo was very blue and lonely. These men and their wives came together for a little memory circle in front of Levi's tent. They brought olives, and salad, and cheese and bread and wine. They passed their time talking about Delilah. They talked and laughed about how much she loved Philo, and how good he was to her.

Any hour of any day might find one or more of these men sitting in this circle. It was sacred ground to them, and everyone was welcome. When Jesus began to join the group regularly, everyone welcomed him. Even if he was a regular attender at the synagogue, he was welcome.

Even if he healed occasionally, as so many others claimed for themselves, Jesus was welcome. He could relax at the sinners' and tax collector's tent, as they commonly called it.

This did not work the other way around. Levi and Philo were not really welcome at the synagogue. Levi collected taxes for the government, so almost everyone assumed he was also a cheat and a thief. Philo just rarely went to the synagogue. He felt nothing was there for him. He had a good relationship with the Lord, but he just ignored the synagogue. It held nothing for him.

Occasionally the rabbi an elder said something to Philo about this omission, but Philo just let it pass. The good people of the synagogue just called this bunch of men "sinners." They assumed the men would go to Hades when they come to the ends of their lives.

So when Jesus began to join the group often, the men welcomed him with both surprise and pleasure. In their hearts, they sensed he spoke for the Lord for them in many ways. Jesus talked about openness, and justice, and acceptance, and forgiveness. He talked about purifying the temple, and about healing. These were the calling cards of Galilean Judaism. The phrases spoke of the Sons of Korah and the healing pool of Bethsaida.

Jesus returned the favor by joining the sinners and the tax collector. Some of them razzed him a little. They called him "Holy Man", or "Son of Man." Once or twice someone asked him, with a laugh, if he were the messiah. Most thought this would make him laugh, or would irritate him.

Jesus just smiled. Clearly this was not an insult. Sometimes he said "You have said so. I guess we must all take your word. If you said it, it must be true. You have never lied, have you? So now what will you do?" So Philo threatened to make a little sign out of clay to point out the messiah. Then everyone laughed. Except Jesus. He only smiled.

One day a fellow asked Jesus a simple question. "Jesus, you seem to know a lot about the temple, and about the Lord. Why is it that you spend your time here rather than in the council at the synagogue? Those people would surely understand you and would want to hear what you have to say."

Jesus laughed aloud. With a mischievous grin, he replied. "They could not handle what I have to say. It is like good new wine. If you put new wine in an old wineskin, the wineskin will swell up and burst. Then we will waste the wine."

Jesus picked up one of Philo's new wineskins. "Putting new wine in new skins is better. At least you will not waste the wine."

Slowly, slowly, a miracle came over Philo. He began to

feel a part of the community of faith. He began to sense a relationship with the Lord. He was not ready to name Jesus as the messiah. Not yet. Having this carpenter's son around was good, even if all he did was listen and talk.

So the days passed. Philo and Levi no longer cared if the snooty ones from the synagogue looked down their noses at them. They only cared if they had peace with their Creator. Whenever Jesus came around, that is how he left them. At peace with the Lord, with a skin full of new wine.

Amen

# 37. Purity is Next to Holiness
## Luke 11:37-12:1  Mark 8:11-12
### How do you wash your hands?
### Gospel Time: 335

Jothias' mind wandered silently as he worked. If anyone happened to be watching him, they would think he put all his thought processes into his numbers. As Jothias leaned over his table, he moved his hand only occasionally. His eyes followed the quill as it scratched out column after column of numbers and words.

The synagogue elders had good reasons to entrust their records to Pharisees such as Jothias. Pharisees usually kept careful and complete records. Scribes and Pharisees, Pharisees and scribes. Two classes of faithful Jews trusted by everyone to do very complex work for the government and the synagogue.

The scribes kept records of all matter of personal issues. Copies of ancient scrolls such as Isaiah and Leviticus. Names of persons given appointments or elected to office in the local government or synagogue. Persons listed as unclean by local priests. Exchange of deeds, records of marriage and divorce. Even in the smallest community a scribe kept busy.

Community Pharisees had even broader duties to fulfill. Numbers of people known to be living in the community.

Measures of barley and wheat raised in the fields. Percentages of taxes levied on different families and businesses. Prices of horses and other animals traded among citizens. Copies of bureaucratic decisions concerning land or contracts. Numbers and words. More words and more numbers. Records must be kept of everything.

Jothias was a natural as a Pharisee. After his education by the elders and priests of the community, Jothias spent nearly all his remaining years in service to the government, the synagogue and the temple. Wages were good. Each entry into the books of the scribes and Pharisees cost someone a small fee. It could be barter, such as fish or grain or bread. It could be coins. Both were good in the eyes of the community and the receivers.

More important to Jothias than the income was the support his trade gave to his personal tastes. Whenever he entered some complex issue into the records, his neighbors and friends gave him much personal praise. They thanked him for his fine understanding of community legal matters. They admired his handwriting. The entire community praised his commitment to accuracy.

This repeated praise lifted his spirits and told him he was doing what the Lord wanted him to do. He was making his home town, Chorazin, a better place by his detailed work. Each time someone offered admiring words for his careful handwork, Jothias became more committed to doing his work in the most proper manner. Then others heard about his skill and commitment, and more work came his way. Around and around, his career lifted him to great heights.

As the community recognized Jothias more and more for his skill and commitment, he began to seek out and accept other duties. He began to see himself as a strong leader of the sanhedrin, the local council of elders of the community. No longer did he need to wait until asked by others to question the propriety of the heavy issues of the community. He accepted the task of asking questions first, and judging propriety later.

This careful Pharisee began to take his responsibility even more seriously as years went along. He felt a call to be pure in his home life just as he was pure in his public life. Even the act of purifying his home life gave him more strength for the purity of his synagogue and other community responsibilities.

So Jothias approached every meal in the same manner. He washed his hands in a basin of clean water from the city well. As he washed, he prayed that the Lord would guide his hands to provide pure food for his own mouth and for the mouths of his family.

Then, sitting with his face toward the temple, Jothias prayed. He prayed he would violate none of the ancient dietary laws as he ate this bountiful meal. He prayed to the Lord to use Jothias' hands to provide food to any who might pass his way in hunger. Finally, Jothias spoke carefully his prayer that this food would bless him and his family and guests.

Jothias always sat next to the place reserved for Elijah, the messiah or the uninvited but expected guest. Elijah's cup was always to his right. The cup always held at least a small amount of wine, perhaps just a few drops. The ancient laws said that the cup and bread were to be offered with some leaves and stems of valuable herbs. Mint, dill and cumin grew wild in the area. Jothias went out to the patches which grew these herbs. He brought home a good portion for their own meal. As Shani placed Elijah's cup and the bread, she had some herbs to place with them. This was their tithe of good things to the Lord, given to the uninvited guest.

When Jothias broke the bread, he always carefully and with some show of faith placed a small portion of bread with some herbs on a napkin or plate near the Elijah's cup. This way, if Elijah, the messiah, or some other should come, the guest had food. More could be added, of course. This was the way every meal should be prepared.

But preparing the meal properly was not really Jothias' work. It was a task for Jothias' wife, Shani. Shani very carefully prepared the meal, and placed it just the way Jothias wanted. However, this was not a pleasant task for Shani.

Before and after every meal, Shani let Jothias know she did not believe this extra work was in any way necessary. She threatened to hire some local girl to prepare the Elijah's cup and spread the napkin to receive the bread. These required only about ten seconds of her time with each meal. It was not onerous work. She just did not believe it to be necessary. Before and after every meal, day after day, she told Jothias of her needless work. She never let him forget it. Yammer. Yammer. Even these minutes of tension strengthened Jothias' resolve to keep the ancient mealtime laws.

Shani and Jothias had a son, David. He was nearly old enough to leave home now. He felt about the meal preparations just as did Shani. He mocked his father's efforts to carry out the laws of purity. Every time Shani voice her disapproval of Jothias' faith, David added his negative attitude toward the old faith.

Every day, David promised to forget the old laws as soon as he moved away. There would be food for any uninvited guest. However, David did not feel any need to place the cup and the bread out for just any meal. They could wait until the guest showed up.

Josiah kept the ritual laws as best he could. Every meal, the cup and the bread were in place. Then, after the meal, Jothias prayed again. He primarily reminded the Lord, his family and guests of the careful preparation of the food and the prayers said over it. Everything was good and pure about the meal. Jothias could now go out into the community to take on more extreme issues.

Jothias' responsibility included hearing out traveling preachers as they came through Chorazin. Jothias' home town was only a few miles from Capernaum perhaps ten. The distance to Bethsaida was about eighteen or twenty miles. Because the general route from Egypt to Babylon passed through the area, strangers were very common in all these cities and villages. Nazareth, Capernaum, Tiberias, Bethsaida, Chorazin and Damascus constantly hosted trading caravans, armies, healers and teachers.

Jesus seemed to visit the area frequently. Jesus moved to Capernaum as a young man, then spent several years establishing himself as a carpenter and healer. He often took his work to Bethsaida and Chorazin during those years. It seemed he did more healing in Bethsaida. He found a larger group of folks asking for healing in that resort city.

In Capernaum and Chorazin, Jesus worked more as a carpenter. Neither of these cities had the reputation of healing enjoyed by Bethsaida. Neither had the healing bath pool of Bethsaida. Those waters were known to have miraculous powers.

Jesus worked hard around the area, building up his skills and his reputation. By working around the area, Jesus became something of a local treasure. His skill as a carpenter put him in demand by many people. He could build homes and sheds. He added on rooms, and made furniture. Jesus mended roofs and doors for homes all over the north shore of the Sea of Galilee.

As Jesus worked around the area, his employers usually offered him some portion of their meal. Occasionally it was just bread and wine. Sometimes he had fruit and fish. The food was always good. Many times he drank from Elijah's cup and ate the offered bread and herbs.

Jesus worked for Jothias and Shani several days repairing a portion of their roof. Each day, a small mid-day meal was part of the package. Each day Jesus washed his hands according to the law. Then he waited, watched and prayed as Jothias proceeded through his own ritual of faith.

One day Jesus went with Jothias on a little walk to harvest a new supply of herbs. Jothias simply entered any patch where he found the herbs growing. He made no effort to purchase the herbs from the garden owners. He just picked the herbs.

This practice was an old tradition among the Jews. A Pharisee, in the employ of the synagogue, could legally harvest certain fruits and herbs from any garden for his own use. Of course, rarely did any Pharisee harvest from the home of a powerful family. This might mean trouble for the Pharisee. Jesus noticed this pattern. He had seen it before, but expected better from Jothias.

Jesus and Jothias ate their mid-day meal quietly. Afterward, Jesus sat in the cool shade to let his lunch satisfy him. Jothias, however, took the time to complete his ritual meal practices. He washed his hands carefully again. The prayers after the meal came easy to him.

As he washed his hands, he noticed Jesus made no effort to satisfy the laws. When he finished, Jothias challenged Jesus on the matter. "Jesus, I do not understand. You can see that I try to follow the law of our people. I am very careful to wash my hands and pray before and after every meal. Shani and I have Elijah's cup, bread and herbs out for every meal. We are very careful to follow the law this way."

"I know you, too, are careful about the law. I have seen you wash your hands and pray before each meal. But I noticed, today, that you did not wash and pray after the meal. You know that is required of us by the law. It is a matter of cleanliness and righteousness. We must live as the law requires. It is a matter of faith, as well as law. Why, Jesus, why?"

Jesus smiled pleasantly at Jothias. "My friend, you are correct. It is a matter of inner cleanliness. Faith is also a matter of righteousness and justice. However, who lives a more just and righteous life? Is it the one who washes his or her hands after the meal? Or is it the one who deals in righteous and justice with neighbors, and the poor?"

Jothias paused a moment before answering. "When did you ever see me deny justice to anyone? You know I have tried to follow the law every day of my life. Everyone who knows me knows I try to be just and righteous with everyone."

"I have never participated in stoning any person except those condemned by the law. Never. I have never voted with the elders to whip any except those who deserve it. Again, according to the law. I have never even participated in the slave market. I do not even hold a slave. I never have, and I never shall. So why do you accuse me of lawlessness?"

Now Jesus' face grew darker. "Jothias, my friend, there are big things and little things. Both are important. The law says that all must be dealt with properly."

Jesus went on, more quietly. "So tell me, Jothias, which is more important? Is it a large thing, such as taking herbs from the gardens of the poor? Or is it assuming that those least able to give , even to the Lord, are the most vulnerable to your wandering hands? Should they be forced by a Pharisee to give the most to you and your family? You have plenty. Can you not grow your own herbs in your own garden?"

"Or is it a small thing, such as washing your hands after a meal. Is it washing your hands after a simple meal when you never got so much as a crumb on your hands? Is that more important than giving justice to the poor?"

Jothias seemed astonished he was being charged with injustice. Not only that, but the person making the charge was a barely literate carpenter. This man had nothing to his name but some carpentry tools, a few articles of clothing and a piece of a copy of the scroll of Isaiah, with a few psalms.

But Jothias could not push back against the challenge. His personal drive toward righteousness and purity pressed him to take seriously any challenge such as this. He must take seriously any possible opportunity to live the just and righteous life opened to him.

Without a word from his mouth, Jothias picked up the remainders of his meal, along with his quills and writing surfaces, paper and skins. With that, and without a nod to Jesus, he started back to the synagogue to complete his work for the day.

Jesus watched him go, smiled to himself, and went back to the roof. He still had work to do for Josiah and

Shani.  This roof was the other part of his mission for the
day.

## 38. Speedy Ben
<u>John 9:1-41</u>; Psalm 23; 1 Samuel 16:1-13; Ephesians 5:8-
14
Ben tries very hard to be successful.
Two months after Easter      Gospel Time: 340


Ben was late. Benjamin bar Jehuda was very, very late. Perhaps we should say Benjamin bar Jehuda was always late. Always. Usually, Ben was late for life. He just tried to gain the good life for himself and for his family. This service of others took a little extra time..

Ben ran the fish bone comb through his hair, but his mind was someplace else. Then he dashed out the door. He almost kissed the dog and patted his wife on the head. His mind was on something else entirely. He corrected himself quickly. Ben's wife, Martha, appreciated the kiss. Atlas, the dog, wagged her tail, and Ben was off.

As a dust contrail trailed Ben down the street, Martha talked seriously with Atlas. "Atlas, old friend, why is Ben that way? He's always in a hurry. He never knows we are here. He is just so busy making money. I suppose we should be thankful for the money. Sometimes, though, I wish he could slow down a little."

Today, Ben had a good day. Ben traded a milking nanny goat for four lambs. Then he traded the lambs for a silver goblet. He traded the goblet for four colorful robes. Then he swapped the robes for a young camel. He immediately bargained the camel for an ox cart loaded with flour. He did not have any oxen.

Because he did not have oxen to pull the cart, Ben puzzled for a moment. Then he traded the cart and flour for six nanny goats and their seven kids. This master merchant was very happy. An increase of twelve live goats in one day. That is sharp trading and great work.

Ben came home that night to feel good about his achievements. He brought home to his wife not just one nanny goat but thirteen goats. He brought one milking nanny goat and six more milking nanny goats. Well, and their seven kids. Ben and Martha did not have time to milk the nannies. Oh, well. The kids will take care of that.

For some reason, Martha was not very happy with the prize. "Get those stupid goats out of the beds. If one of those bawling boneheads messes up my house, that is it! It will not be their hide drying on the rack tomorrow. It will be yours, Benjamin bar Jehuda."

"All day long I try to fix up the house just for you. I cook your meals and make your clothing. I clean the beds and clean the floors. Then you come in late at night bringing in thirteen four-legged garbage disposals. They eat what I have fixed for you and me. Then you say `What is for supper?'."

"What is the matter? Is my food so bad you choose not to eat it? You choose to bring home a flock of goats to eat the food I prepare! Is that because you are too proud to eat it?"

"You have not seen the grandchildren for a month. They do not live so far away that you need to bring home substitutes. They could come and cuddle with you or play with you. Your own kin sometimes would like to talk to you. That is more than these stupid goats will ever do."

"You ignore the children. Are you too rich for children? Your own son and his children live on the other end of this house. Have you forgotten them? You must have. You have not seen any of them in daylight in months, or is it years?"

"Did you know you have a grandson? He was born some time back, you know. He's dating now."

The words just kept going on, and going on, on and on. A torrent of abuse swept toward this poor man. He had thought he was gaining on the good life. He had believed himself to be meeting some kind of success. Maybe not. Finally Ben could take the abuse no longer. Now with a bitter heart, he left the house.

He slowly walked out into the cold Galilean hills, shivering from the cold night air. Alone again that night, he was cold, miserable, mad and frustrated.

All the next day Ben stayed out in the hills. High on the

bluff, his eyes and his heart searched for truth. Ben studied the stars, wondering just what to do. This was not a day for trading or preparing a sales pitch. He just wrestled with himself and wondered what to do.

Early next morning Ben's oldest grandson found Ben sleeping fitfully in a small cave. Huddled down in the ground for shelter against the cold, Ben shielded himself. He hid from the weather, and his own world, as well.

"Grandpa Ben! Wake up! Are you all right? We have looked all night for you."

"Yes, Jonathan, I'm all right. I just had to have time alone to think."

"Grandpa, I heard a man talking yesterday. I think you should talk to him. I know you and Grandma are having some problems between you. This man talked about how to make life right and good. You can find him today down by the city gate. His name is Jesus. Go listen to him. Please, Grandpa?"

Jonathan did not follow Ben down the hill immediately. He stood still, but the pleading sound of Jonathan's voice stayed in Ben's heart. He wondered about this fellow Jesus. Maybe he had some advice. Ben was just about at the end of his rope. Something had to change, and change quickly.

If he could just find this Jesus, perhaps Ben had hope. Maybe Ben could learn the secret to the good life. Just his hope seemed to give Ben a quicker step. Jesus should be at the gate, so he walked toward the wall.

Ben saw a crowd at the gate. It seemed they were beginning to break up. Oh, no, he could not be so close to healing and be frustrated. To be disappointed because he was late would be too much. He could see his only possibility disappearing just as he came close. Now on a dead run, Ben reached the crowd.

He pushed people out of the way. As he ran, he stepped on the hands and feet of children on the ground. Ignoring their protests and cries, he pushed in. Desperately trying to get near Jesus, he pushed hard. He was not concerned for a moment with the children. He had to find the key to the good life.

"Rabbi! Rabbi! Before you leave, tell me what I have to do to find peace? What do I have to do to have the good life? What are the words I have to say? Do I need to give money? Please, Jesus, I have heard you are a good man, a holy man. Please, I beg you, what do I need to do?"

Jesus waited a moment for Ben to finish his plea. Jesus looked Ben in the eye. Ben saw in his mind's eye his wife, his children and his grandchildren.

Then Jesus said "You must give away to the poor all you own. Then follow me!"

Speedy Ben walked away. He was now a very sad man.

# 39. Foxes, Birds and Disciples
Matthew 8:19-22; Matthew 8:19-22, Luke 9:57-62
Jesus recalls his days herding sheep as he
lays out the meaning of discipleship.
Gospel Time: 350

The little fire made a warm glow on the eager faces gathered around. Little groups of men and women talked quietly among themselves. The last of the evening light disappeared slowly beyond the west Galilean hills. The evening breeze was dying, slowing to about the speed a person could walk. It would be just enough to give a person in a bedroll some comfort in the early evening. Then, as the night grew colder, the breeze would finally ease to a stop.

When the breeze quit, every person in the camp shivered a bit. Then each pulled the bedclothes more tightly around, and tried to go back to sleep. Most of this crowd did not know it yet, but little sleep would come on this night. Some would get no sleep at all.

Andrew and the other disciples stood impatiently as they waited in the evening firelight. Jesus was going around the circle, speaking softly to little groups of his people. After he moved on, those he just left either stood silently or began to talk nervously about Jesus' words.

Wherever he went, Jesus obviously had critical news for the group.

Those who still waited for Jesus to come to them obviously knew what the news concerned. They watched him move around, speak briefly with a small group, then move on. Sometimes after Jesus moved on, the little group would re-mix with other small groups. Sometimes the little group of two or three just stood together or sat on rocks or stumps around the fire.

Once Jesus spoke with a group, and moved on, the real work seemed to begin. A new focus seemed to appear for each in the waning light of day. Jesus, himself, seemed excited about the new step for his ministry. He was sending two or three of the followers to each village around the Sea of Galilee.

Some little groups of two or three were going to towns right on the shore. Bethsaida, Gennesaret, Tiberias and Gergesa seemed the most inviting to some. That was fine. Others were going to settlements a few miles from this comforting body of water. Sennabis, Saab, Ptolemais and Gaddara were just some of the intended recipients of Jesus' mission.

Part of the exciting news for the group came as Jesus announced his plans for his future ministry. None among the group gave a thought to another possibility. That is, that Jesus' plans might change along the way. It had already happened, at least once. Some disciples had gone to Gammala to prepare the town for Jesus' arrival.

When they arrived in Gammala, they met with the elders at the city gate. Their mission was to tell the elders of Jesus' impending arrival. After only a few minutes of discussion, and a couple questions, an elder spoke for all of them.

"We have heard of this Jesus. He came from Nazareth to become part of the healing and tourism industry of Bethsaida and Capernaum. We have heard he is a good healer; we give him credit for that much. True, some people here need healing."

"We have a problem with your Jesus. He makes big crowds wherever he goes. People get excited. They think he is going to heal the blind. Or they think maybe he will walk on water, or disappear before their very eyes, or turn water into wine. Maybe he would. We just do not think so."

"Even if he did those things, it would take away all our business. Everyone would leave the market place. People would be too busy talking. They would not spend their money, or do any trading with the shop keepers. They would give Jesus their money rather than give it to the synagogue or buy sacrifices with it. We would have a terrible problem."

"No, we think it would not be good for Jesus to come

to Gammala at this time. We probably not protect him from our own people. Maybe in a few years, he might come. If he proves he is not a danger to Gammala, and our businesses, perhaps he can eventually come. Not right now. Mind you, there is nothing personal about this. You will surely understand. We hold nothing personal about this. We just do not trust him or you."

When this news reached Jesus, a little earlier today, Jesus and the others were already nearing Gammala. With just a couple small settlements and a few hours between Jesus and Gammala, the word came to change course. The only road to take was the road back west to the Sea of Galilee.

Jesus turned back after the disappointment. Because it was late in the afternoon, he opted to make it only to the first settlement. It straddled the wadi road going back to the Sea of Galilee. The little group had a small well in the wadi. This well provided sufficient water for the travelers and the families who lived there. The local had welcomed Jesus on his first visit. The second visit was just as welcome. These people had very few visitors who came their way anytime. However, they recognized the purchasing power of a few dozen men and women. The locals brought out bread, berries, olives, figs and other goodies for the guests. All this was available for a price, of course.

Now, in the late evening, everyone had eaten well and picked their soft, sandy bed-spots for the night. Some wanted the soft sand in the wadi. Others wanted the dusty area above the wadi, on the flat land.

A few had blisters or bruises to attend. Others needed some special cleaning and fresh oil applied on rashes and dry skin. Olive and fish oil, alternated with lanolin, did a great work of salving red and broken skin.

By the time the sun was completely down, Jesus' moving crowd had taken care of their cleanliness and health. They gathered again around the little fire in the wadi. Relaxed, now, they regained strength from the food, water and rest. They stood in clumps, or knelt, or sat close in the area. This was the group, now, which could take on all the ups and downs of Jesus' mission to Galilee. They would spread from the Decapolis to Caesarea Philippi, and from Capitolias to Tyre.

Jesus was ready. He was prepared, and he knew his people were ready. They could make the next step in his mission to the north country, Galilee. His planning and preparation included sending small groups to the communities he had chosen to visit in the future. He would do this regularly in his ministry after this initial assignment.

Jesus seemed to have these assignments pre-arranged in his mind as he went around the circle in the wadi. Some communities were completely unexpected to the assigned visitors. Others were obvious choices. Abela and Gadara made sense. Large communities, with strong leadership. Rumah and Sepph made no sense at all. Just a few people, extremely poor and getting worse. Neither even had a functioning synagogue.

Sometimes the disciples just did not understand people in the villages around the Sea of Galilee. By now, Jesus was well known around Galilee. Everyone should have known about Jesus, his healing, his teaching, his traveling group. After all, he had made crippled men and women and children walk. He made the blind see. He made the deaf hear. He had a large group of people traveling with him, needing shoes, clothing, food, medicine, and other valuable supplies. They were a great boon for those who bought and sold in the market place. Many Galileans acted as if they knew nothing about him. Strange.

Jesus began his evening pep talk to his people with a smile. These folks were tired, and deserved some good words to keep them strong. They were committed to Jesus, but fatigue can take a terrible toll.

So Jesus first simply stood in the circle as his people stood around near him. A few sat after their long day's trek.

Jesus smiled. "Are your feet tired? Mine are. I got a little rock between my toes today. I didn't notice it until I

had walked a good distance. I guess I can live with it."
He smiled again.

"Please do not worry about the problem with Gammala.
That stuff happens. We are here now, and that is good.
Do not worry about me. Foxes have holes in the ground
for rest. Birds of the air have nests in the ground. The Son
of Man has nowhere to lay his head. So relax tonight, my
friends. We have a long way to go tomorrow." As he
finished, all the group stood, as if expecting some sort of
closing statement.

Now Jesus began his tour of the little groups of men
and women as they waited for his individual word. A
common practice of Jesus strengthened his ties with them.
He liked to have a special word for each person traveling
with him just before they closed the day. Now Jesus went
from group to group. This time, however, everyone knew
something different was passing between Jesus and the
people. After Jesus left each group, the little groups
changed attitude, found new partners to talk with, or just
fell silent. They just changed.

So that is how Jesus announced his plans to his people.
He gave them assignments, and rewarded them with
responsibility and with praise. He showed his confidence
in their ability to carry out their work.

As he went around the group, Jesus met some minor
resistance  only once. He said to Elias, "I want you to stay

near me. I want you to walk where I walk, and help me along the way."

Elias responded. "Uuhhh, Jesus, I want very much to do that. However, my grandmother is near death. I need to spend some time at home, to tell her good-bye. Then I will come be with you forever."

Jesus looked at Elias again. "Do you really believe you will not see her again? No one who puts his hand to the plow and looks back is fit for the kingdom of God."

Jesus used this process of telling everyone their assignments for other work as well. Jesus made clear which of the group he wanted to walk with him as a close disciple. These would walk closely with Jesus, visiting, healing, teaching, organizing. It was a position of honor, but also a position of hard work.

In the morning as everyone ate their breakfast and prepared to leave, Jesus went a little way from the group. He knelt, obviously in prayer. No one heard his words, but they all knew he was praying for his people as they left. Some of them might never return. Some might face terrible danger. So Jesus prayed.

When Jesus returned to the group, Jesus was ready to give his final instructions. "Listen. I am sending you out to do my work. You are going as sheep in a wolf pack. So be smart as snakes and pure as doves. Take no money, gold or silver or copper with you. You will not need extra clothing, sandals, anything. If some town closes you out, shake their dust out of your sandals, and move on."

"Preach to anyone who will listen. Tell them the kingdom of heaven is here. Heal the sick, raise the dead. Do what I would do. I am praying for you."

When Jesus finished sending his people to their assignments, everyone started away. Most on the road. Some across between roads. All headed intently to experience the kingdom of heaven on earth.

Amen.

# 40. Scythopolis
Luke 10:1-20; Psalm 30; 2 Kings 5:1-14; Galatians 6:1-16
Jesus sends the seventy away,
then asks them to return to meet with him.
July 3-9      Gospel Time: 360


The second dozen around Jesus thought they did all the work. They were a little frustrated the first dozen got most of the credit.

One of this second twelve was an ordinary fellow. Elos worked very hard. He saw himself as committed totally to Jesus. Elos was just not as well known as some others.

Jesus sent the second twelve out, each with a mission. They went off to all the towns in the north of Palestine and into Lebanon. Most of the first twelve stayed close. They may have felt the need to stay in touch. Perhaps Jesus felt a need to have them close for training or building the community.

A few stayed close to Jesus for special contingencies. Some catastrophe such as the end of the world could come at any moment. Several were always prepared to spend the next few days in prayer.

Jesus sent the second twelve to the farther towns. Many of them never returned. These were victims of accidents, or disease, or repression. Some were unable to keep the faith. A few missionaries just stayed on in their new locations, working for Jesus.

After Jesus finished giving everyone else their assignments, he looked at Elos for a moment. Everyone knew Jesus had something special in his mind for Elos. His eyes squinted as he thought carefully before he spoke.

"Elos, I have a challenge for you. Everyone else is going out two at a time to spread the kingdom. Some of our people are going north to Damascus. Several are headed for Jerusalem, or for Egypt. Some are going over into the Decapolis. Everyone has their own assignment now except you."

"I have not forgotten you. I have a special task for you. This work means a lot to me. I know you can do it."

"The little town called Scythopolis has asked for someone to come in my name. I want you to go there. You already know what to do. I have watched you work."

"The problem is I do not have anyone to send with you. I had hoped someone else might come along, but no one has. Are you willing to go by yourself? Do you believe you can handle it?"

"Scythopolis!" thought the dumbstruck Elos. "Scythopolis! No one wants to go to Scythopolis. Good grief! I can not go there. They resent even their own prophets there. They had another prophet who went to Scythopolis a few months ago. They strung him up on a tree. The last prophet who went there failed miserably. He only went to announce a new world. The people saw to it his new world lasted only a few days. Some priests put a crown of thorns on his head and called him the King." The image dancing in Elos' head panicked him for a moment.

The stream of confused thoughts continued. "I can not do it. I am afraid. I do not know what to do. I am too young to die. Go alone? Why me? Send me to Tyre or Sidon. If I fail there, I can just get on a ship and keep on going. Send me to Babylon so I can be a slave. I can go to Egypt to build another pyramid in my captivity. Still, Scythopolis? Forget it, buster!" thought Elos.

"Jesus, uuuhhhh, I think I need to pray about this. It is very difficult, you know. I hear strong persons are there who are pretty set in their ways. They are all Samaritans. Every one of them. Samaritans do not take kindly to outsiders. They carry long knives. My mother told me I should not marry a Samaritan. I do not know the language all that well. I hear tales of a high cost of living there."

Jesus laughed. "Elos, I am not sending you to Scythopolis to build a harem. Anyone can produce a large family. No, people there need me. I just can not go every place and talk to every person."

"Go to Scythopolis and you will find the wildest thing. The people there are just ordinary folk. Teachers and rabbis and homemakers and children. The mayor is a decent chap, although he is getting on in years. You will meet a psychologist who has a son. He is spoiled rotten."

"When you go to the inn, tell them I sent you. They will put you up. Free. They have promised me this. Just go, and tell them about me. That's all you have to do. Will you go?"

Jesus really did not give Elos a chance to say "No!" Before Elos knew what was up, he was on his way south. He wandered slowly to the little Samaritan town of Scythopolis. As he came near the ancient Greek city he had a strange feeling. He felt he had been part of this scene before.

It was just as Jesus had described the town. So much so that Elos suspected Jesus had been there to make the arrangements. That had to happen during one times Jesus just disappeared for several days. Elos found teachers and rabbis with their funny little black hats.

Elos met the mayor, a decent chap. He clearly expected Jesus to send someone. The mayor probably expected someone with a higher status in the organization. The mayor was getting old, was gray and too plump to be a great politician.

His honor, the mayor, introduced Elos to the chief rabbi in town. This highly respected man also served as a community counselor. That rabbi was busy writing a grant so he could attend a conference at Tyre. He needed to spend a few days training in new methods. He could also catch a few rays of ocean front sunshine.

The counselor's son kept interrupting the conversation. Finally he kicked Elos in the shin and screamed at everyone. "Get out of here! I want to talk now!"

The mayor took Elos to the inn. This was a comfortable facility run by Jacob with help from a woman called Elissa. Elissa had been a dressmaker. As her eyes failed she had to find other work. The inn was the only available work in town.

Late in the evening, Jacob provided a meal of mutton stew for Elos. After Elos ate, Jacob showed Elos the corner of the room where he could sleep.

Scythopolis once had a fairly heavy traffic of commercial travelers. Now few people came through the town. The commercial travelers all slept on the floor on straw pallets in the big room. During the day the pallets were picked up and piled neatly in the corner.

Straw pallets attracted many mice, and mice attracted cats. Jacob whispered to Elos he wanted to get rid of some cats, but Elissa refused. She said they needed the cats to keep the mouse population down. Still, forty-'leven cats?

Elos' feet were so tired he really did not care about many cats around. He just wanted to sleep. He did not even care if half the travelers and dogs in the place snored. Nothing could be worse than James and John, the sons of thunder. However, he did appreciate the cat that curled itself up at his feet. The warmth felt good, and he was soon fast asleep.

Suddenly a man jumped violently and roared in the dim lamplight. His actions started everything going. Dogs panicked and started fighting. Cats scattered. Elos sat up in a daze and wondered whether to panic and run. He knew, he just knew, he should not have come. The light from the tiny lamp burned through the night. It only allowed some sense of forms jumping and moving around in confusion.

Finally the voice of the man who had started the confusion came strong and clear. "Settle down. Go back to sleep. That blasted cat just licked the bottom of my foot. Good . . . night."

Elos learned to put up with the cats. Elissa was very kind and made it worth the trouble. When Elos went out into the town, he tried to follow Jesus' style. He often found someone who was hungry or sleeping under the bridge. At first Elos begged the merchants around town to help him provide for the poor. They soon tired of the drain on their purses. He began to bring them back to the inn for food. Elos offered to go without a meal or a place to sleep. Elissa usually cared for the stranger somehow.

Dear Elissa provided a bath, and some food. Through much of the night Elos, Jacob and Elissa just talked. Some others who could not sleep sat and visited quietly. They talked mostly about taking some steps helping the poorest become leaders of the community.

The process seemed long and hard, harder even than Elos had feared. Elos doubted he was doing any good in Scythopolis. He tried and tried. He talked to every person he could find. Only by scouring the streets did he find interested people. He talked to rabbis, and homemakers, and merchants, and children. Elos tried everything he could imagine. He succeeded only in growing more dis-couraged as time went on.

Finally the time came to report to Jesus about Scythopolis. Elos knew from experience Jesus will take the time to listen to a full report. Jesus will want to know what great things he had done for Scythopolis. Jesus will ask how many lives Elos had renewed.

Elos were most embarrassed when he thought he had wasted his time. He had spent much time trying to help the poor people of Scythopolis live. That was probably good. He helped them find food and shelter and new life. His shame was he had not built any organization. He had not really spent much time talking about Jesus. Now he had no time.

Elos needed to take someone with him. He had no other

witness. He needed to prove he had not just been standing around. He thought of all those he had tried to help. In frustration he panicked, knowing well that apparently he had not really helped anyone.

Several alcoholics had gone back to the jug. Some of his projects had just wandered off. These kings of the road had no desire to stay in town for anything. Some had just come in for the bath and for the food. When the sun came up, they were on the road again. It was very frustrating for Elos.

Elos now must go back north to Jesus and admit his failure. He sat on the inn steps, discouraged. He sat outside the inn with his head in his hands. Elissa came and sat beside him. "Elos, what is the problem? I thought you were excited about going back to the Sea of Galilee. I thought you wanted to see Jesus and your old friends again. You are moping around here as if you do not really want to go. What is it?"

Elos talked to Elissa about standing in the gathering of Jesus and admitting his failure. He could not see he had helped anyone find a new life. Everything in town looked pretty much as it did on the day he came.

Elos and Elissa sat in the cool evening talking and watching the stars. They wondered what might have been if they had some money. Maybe if Jesus could have sent someone with Elos. They talked about all those with whom they had worked. They talked about their hopes for successes in the future. Elos had little to claim as success tonight. As the evening went on, at least Elos had talked to someone about his problems. Maybe he would get some sleep that night.

Finally, after a long period of silently listening and thinking, Elissa spoke softly. "May I go with you? I want to be there when you speak. I'd like to meet this Jesus you talk so much about. I am sure Jacob will let me have a few days off. The cats will be all right."

Elos laughed. This was not exactly what he had expected. Elissa? Hardly a new person. Hardly one who made major changes in the direction of her life. Elissa was a good woman. She was not one who had seen a new light, ethically and morally. Elos could not brag to Jesus about changing Elissa's place in the community. Changes in Elissa would never prove the work of Elos in Scythopolis.

Elissa was always good company while they walked. If only she did not bring all those blasted cats. A journey with even one cat would be pure disaster. It was no less a struggle than arguing theology with the Sons of Thunder.

Two days later the two were in Capernaum in the evening, down by the lake. Jesus was there with the disciples and the rest of the second twelve. The word spread Jesus was calling his people together for a meeting. Some curious folks came out from town to learn whatever they could about Jesus. Some wanted to support the work. These just came along to be helpful in whatever way they could. Some came expecting some kind of miracle.

Jesus asked the disciples to stay with the crowd. Then the second twelve should come away from the crowd with him. He wanted to be with them, to talk privately with them. He needed to pray with them.

Some disciples pointed out the hungry crowd. Most of the people had not eaten for several hours. Only one small boy packed a lunch. A few biscuits and a couple fish were all the food available.

Jesus took these simple foods, blessed them, and handed them to the disciples. "Here, take this food, and feed the people. Then come join the rest of us. Bring what you have left with you. We will be up by that rock." Jesus pointed to a large boulder on the hill.

Jesus took the second twelve off by themselves. He needed to talk with them about their work. The disciples gasped at Jesus' orders. They grumbled some, but began to serve the people the bit of food available. Jesus and his people gathered near the rock. He asked the men and women feeding the people how they could feed so many.

A couple had been to Tiberias. They cast out demons in the name of the Lord. Two had just recently returned from Sidon. Their mission was among the Roman garrison there. On and on it went. It seemed each person had a more successful story to tell.

Finally, at last, only Elos had not spoken. Jesus turned to Elos. "I sent you to Scythopolis to feed my sheep. What happened to you there? Tell us all the great things you have accomplished."

Elos hung his head. He tried to gather his courage to admit failure. A voice beside him spoke clearly. "Let me answer for Elos. He is very bashful just now. My name is Elissa. I can say what Elos cannot find words to say."

"I am a simple woman. All my adult life I have lived alone until just recently. I have made a few shekels sewing clothes for the wealthy. I have even sewed for the poor in Scythopolis. I made a small profit at it."

"My friends have been my cats. We had more cats than we could count. My pay for sewing for the poor has usually been in fish. I have fed the fish to my cats--or any cats who came to me. They have been my family."

"Not long ago I began to lose my sense of touch. I could not sew. The needle did not hold in my hand. I found work cleaning and cooking and keeping accounts at the inn of a friend."

"I was lost. I was lost in a job I did not understand. I did not want to do that job. The people who came in were tired and cranky from travel. They were dirty from the dust of the road. They smelled like camels and donkeys and dogs and cattle. I did not think I could do the work. I knew I did not want to do the work. I was ready to quit the job. I could just wander off in the desert and die."

"Elos came to town and stayed at the inn a few days. One night he brought someone else with him. Elos paid for a bath and food for this fellow. The next night the guest was a different man. Then it was an elderly woman, and many others. I wondered about Elos, whether he knew what he was doing."

"One night he came to me with a problem. He asked for some way to work off the baths and the food. We arranged some things. Every night for the next three weeks, someone else came, asking for help. I began to look forward to the evening, wondering who might come with Elos."

"Each night he came to the door with a frustrated look in his eyes. Sometimes he was apologetic. When he asked for help for his new friend, I cringed. I always gave him a hard time. I always said `Not again!'."

"I began to enjoy helping. I began to enjoy life again. I began to hear the birds sing. I stopped to watch little children play."

As Elissa talked beside him, Elos watched her only in his heart. He remembered the many hours of talking with her. He recalled the strength she seemed to pour into his soul to keep him going. Now he could clearly see her face in his heart's eye. She spoke words he could not find.

"When Elos said he had to come tell you about his failure, I cried. He was embarrassed. He was frustrated. Nevertheless, I am here to say he did not fail!" Everyone heard the new power in her voice.

"I knew he had not failed. He had not failed because at least he changed me. My life was entirely new. I have new hope."

"Jesus, you changed Elos. You changed his life into something new, and exciting, and wonderful. When you did, you changed my life."

"So I had to come, because Elos did not know how he changed my life. He came to Scythopolis just for me. People there needed you, but you never saw them. He came to Scythopolis for me. It is through him I know you, Jesus."

Elos felt the tears running down his cheeks, but no one saw them. Just then disciples came up the hill to Jesus and the second twelve.

"These baskets are full with the leftover food. We still have enough for everyone here. We do not understand. We started with just a little bit, and just fed people. Now we have more than we did when we started. We do not understand."

Jesus smiled and replied "I think Elissa does. I think

Elissa understands."

# 41. Ten Just
Matthew 7:1-4; Luke 6:27-42
Psalm 37:1-11; Genesis 45:3-15; 1 Corinthians 15:35-50
Jesus helps a young mother face a brutal community judge.
February 18-24    Gospel Time: 370

Samantha thought she was used to it now. Her twins played on the ground, half naked. They squabbled in the way of children. They cried, pushed and then laughed with each other. They were good at making each other cry and then making each other laugh. The older women at the community even empathized with Samantha.

"Oh, Lord, you can be thankful they are not old enough to talk yet."

Samantha knew what always came next. "He hit me!" "Mommy!" "Mommy!" "I'm hungry."

The thought of what was coming as the children grew frightened her. Until now she always pushed it out of her mind. Now as the time moved along, these fears stubbornly blurred her vision of the future. They did not go away.

The smell of hot bread lifted her a little. Pulling bread from the community oven always filled her senses. She managed to pinch off a bite of hot bread. She laid the loaf in the shade to cool as she let the children play. The day was too young to focus on the bitterness of her own life.

Nevertheless, the sun already blazed so hot no one sat along the streets. Only village women coming to the community oven to bake braved the heat. Baking bread on such a day was so bad Samantha's head hurt from the heat. She had no choice. She had to feed her children somehow.

The other women knew things were rough with Samantha. Her headaches and trouble with the children had everyone's focus. Neighbors just did not know how to help her in her agony. Sympathetic friends tried to offer advice when they could. Samantha tried to follow their advice, but nothing worked.

Whenever any prophet or a teacher came to the village, he had one specific task. A women always talked to the teacher about Samantha. Usually the answer was the same. "Our Lord is punishing her for abusing the children. She must obey her husband and stop abusing the children. Then the Lord will no longer punish her."

Samantha herself could go without eating. Sometimes she did, several days at a time. Starving herself was not the result of having no food to eat. The pain came from wanting something even more vital to life.

Her husband was gone now. This trading trip took him across the Nile River into Egypt. He was gone two or three months doing his work. Then he was back with Samantha and the children for a couple weeks. He did a good job of providing for the family. For Samantha, this was not enough. She needed him at home now.

Oh, her head hurt. The pain erupted behind the eyes and bored in until pain nearly blinded her. This had happened before, often. Samantha knew what was coming next. She just did not know what to do about it.

Samantha put a wet rag on her head, but this only helped a little while. The children started crying again, which made  a neighbor's dog bark. The sounds seemed to make hash of her brain. Then the fire-pain ran around her head like a crown of thorns. It jammed the pain down into her skull. It made Samantha sick to her stomach. Samantha knew she was losing control.

Just then the kids grabbed her legs. Teasing and playing tag around her aching frame, they laughed and yelled. She slapped each of the giggling children across the face. This made them cry, so she tossed them onto their beds. They lay there terror-stricken again, crying and quivering. Their eyes locked onto their mother in fear she might take offense yet another time.

Samantha threw a loaf of bread on the bed with them. They began to tear it apart to eat. Then she turned to lie in the corner. She huddled in a blanket with the shame of her actions and her pain.

Samantha's ears shut out the pitiful cries of the children now. She drifted off into a half coma, half sleep. This is even nearer to death than life for some. It is almost as welcome. She found in her sleep an unsteady respite for a life coming undone.

For Samantha, the respite did not last long. The tired mother began to dream in the shade of her home. Her mind filled her dreams with the sounds of children crying. Every part of each dream story is the same. Children cry. It was as if her heart tried to flush away the hurts of the day. In her mind's eye she saw herself hitting her children repeatedly. Her soul trembled with terror at her own vicious action.

Samantha cried as she woke and remembered the dream. She held her eyes shut and tried to pray for help. She had tried to pray before, really tried. Her friends and the rabbi had told her how to pray. "You must use the proper words when you pray. You must use the correct words and be totally sincere. Then the Lord will answer your prayers. You will be all right. You will not hurt again. The Lord will take care of you."

So Samantha tried to pray again. She huddled in the corner with her ragged blanket. She started with words that seemed appropriate, but not quite right. "O Lord of life, Creator . . . "

As she prayed, a man's voice from the street interrupted

her words and her thoughts.

"Justice! Justice! Where is our justice? Oh, but we are as bad as Sodom. The Lord will destroy us because we deserve it. He could not find ten just people. I call the community to justice!"

"Justice! Remember Sodom! Help us find ten just people. Surely some people here follow the Law!"

Samantha ran to the door of her house. "Shut up, you crazy man! Shut up. You'll wake my children. Do not say another evil word!" Her headache exploded again behind her eyes.

The street prophet welcomed the challenge. "How dare you speak that way to Xardos, a prophet of the Lord?! I, Xardos, will tell the world about you! You, Samantha, are the worst of the lot! I know about you! You are a child-abuser. You beat on your children for no reason at all! Your mind has no control over your own life. You claim it is because you have headaches. The Lord will punish you until you stop whatever sin it is you have! Do you abuse your children? Is that your sin? Do you cheat on your husband while he is away? Is that your sin? Whatever it is, you will go to Hades for your sin!"

Samantha sank back into her room in tears. The prophet of the Lord moved on down the street. He felt no compassion for the troubled mother. Xardos was completely satisfied in his own righteousness.

Xardos kept up his cry, "Justice! Remember Sodom! Remember, the Lord knows about us. In Sodom, not even fifty righteous were found in the great city. We are worse even than that! Send out your righteous ones. We must prove our nation!"

Xardos made great noise in the town, but no one answered him. No one said he was wrong. Maybe they were afraid. Maybe he was right. Maybe they were afraid he was right.

Xardos loudly worked his way along the street. As he did, a man who attracted a small crowd made his way toward Xardos. Soon Xardos and Jesus stood face to face. Xardos nearly sang his refrain.

"Are you a just man? Are you at one with the Lord? Righteous? Will the Lord destroy us because you, alone, will not be righteous? Answer me, stranger, will you be a just man?"

Jesus smiled and started to answer, but one of the crowd spoke first. "Xardos, you nut, this is Jesus of Nazareth! He's much more a prophet of the Lord than you are. He is a very just man. Perhaps he is the most just man in the world!"

Xardos stood silently for a moment. The crowd buzzed with anticipation at what Xardos might say or do. Jesus only smiled an easy smile and waited.

"Well, whoop-ti-doooo! He claims to be just! Jesus,

what makes you think you are such a just man? Do you keep all the laws perfectly? I know I do."

"Do you read the Torah faithfully and with understanding? So do I."

"Do you worship at the temple and in the synagogue regularly? Me, too, every day of my life since I was twelve years old."

"Are you free of all contact with sinners? Can you turn away from people with scars on their past? Do you avoid gentiles? How about women in their time? Do you avoid lepers? Can you walk away from cripples?"

"If you are a just man, save us from the fate of Sodom. Save us from destruction. Save us from the fires of Hell."

"You can do it if you are a just man. Just help me find eight more like you and me! The Lord has told me to find ten men in this village who are just. We need to support those who follow the Law. Then the Lord will not ravage the town."

As Xardos talked faster, Jesus started walking again, slowly. Xardos backed up but kept talking in Jesus' face. Jesus did not try to answer Xardos. It seemed he had something else on his mind, perhaps another mission. Something was more important than finding ten just men in the city.

Jesus turned to Xardos for a moment. He spoke softly. "It may be what we need is to redeem the town, not just save it."

In a few more minutes Jesus turned toward a home along the street. As he neared the home the crowd noise brought Samantha to the door. Xardos' voice rose above the crowd now as he saw the direction of Jesus' travel.

"That's right! She's the worst of the lot. She walks around with her head in her hands. She does not come out during the day. Maybe she's a witch. She screams at the children and at the men of the Lord. She's at least a child abuser. We have seen her doing things no one ought to do to her own children. Tell her she's a sinner. Tell her she's going to Hades! Her own children will destroy her. You will tell her, Jesus. I know you will. Prove you are a just man! If she screams at you that will prove you are a man of the Lord!"

No one knows just what Jesus said to Samantha. The crowd only saw her head on his chest. Jesus wrapped his arms around her for a moment. Then Jesus reached down and took two little brown children in his arms. The four of them stood in the doorway for a moment before going inside.

Xardos' voice rose with excitement. "Save the children! Save the children! Save them from their mother, the sinner! Save them, Jesus!"

Inside the house, something different was happening. Jesus sat on the straw mat with the children in his arms.

He whispered in their ears and teased their fingers. He sang a little song to them.

While he talked to the children, Samantha brought him a basin of clear, cold water. He used it to bathe his own hands and face.

Jesus took the cloth and water and soon felt much, much cooler. Then Jesus did another pleasant little thing.

Jesus dipped the cloth in the water. Then he washed hands, face and feet of the babies. The carpenter found clean diapers and bathed the little bodies. Somehow the rash from confusion and inattention seemed to just disappear before his touch. Days of grime and dirt disappeared as Jesus simply cared for children.

Samantha began to talk while Jesus bathed her family. Samantha just babbled at first. Soon Samantha was talking about her hurts and her frustrations. She talked about her fears of hurting her children. She wondered about forgiveness from the Lord.

While she talked, Jesus took the little loaf of warm bread from the floor. He gently broke it open for the babies.

Samantha poured out her heart, hardly seeing what Jesus was doing. "I do not know how to pray. I used to try to pray, but I do not remember the words. Nothing seems to work. I want to be right with the Lord, but I do not know how. How can I be a good person, with all the evil I had done? Surely the Lord will not forgive me. Can you help me? Tell me what to do."

Jesus took her hand and held it gently. With easy words, he began to pray for her, quietly.

Outside, Xardos forced his way to the door. As he looked in, his eyes became accustomed to the dark interior. The prophet was aghast at what he saw. He saw this traveling rabbi reaching out and holding the lovely young woman close. This sacred man held a young woman whose husband was gone. He held a young woman who was a terrible sinner. He held a young woman who was an abusive parent. Who could know what else?

"You! Jesus! I expected more out of you! You claim to be a prophet, and I catch you doing this! They said you were a righteous man. You would have been no help in Sodom, and you are no help here. What is the world coming to? They cannot even call the man of the Lord a righteous man! We need ten! We can not even claim this man is one! I did not expect the rest of this rabble to make it, but Jesus! You should have!"

Peter was by now incensed at the man's jury and accusations. Roughly, Peter grabbed him and shoved him away. Peter sent Xardos off up the street still protesting the morals of Jesus.

For a time the silence in the little crowd was a welcome

change. Then Peter and some others came into the room. Jesus rested, at ease with Samantha and the children. Jesus and Samantha sat close together now, each holding a child. Jesus was happy to be together now with this little bit of a family.

Peter waited impatiently. Jesus finally turned to Peter as if to encourage him to speak. "Jesus, I have a question for you now. It is quiet and we have a moment. John taught his disciples how to pray. Could you teach us how to pray?"

Rabbi Jesus looked at the young woman sitting next to him, smiled, and answered, "Sure. When you pray, if your prayer is real, it will be something like this: Father of all, who watches over us from Heaven, your majesty, power and love are truly beyond my understanding. Make this world and all the people live as you want us to live. I want to follow your will on earth as we will follow it in Heaven. Give me bread for today, and make me satisfied with that much. Forgive me when I go against your will. Make me to forgive those who go against your will and hurt me. Lord, keep me away from temptation. Protect me from those who wish to hurt me."

"Now, you can not question whether these are the proper words or thoughts for prayer. You can always say, `This is the way Jesus taught me to pray.'"

Jesus hugged Samantha and her children another time.

Then he took his little crowd and walked on up the street.

# 42. Follow Me
## Mark 13:35-37; Matthew 25:1-13, Luke 12:35-36
### Jesus constantly reaches out for followers
### Gospel Time: 375

Lezar woke early, before the light of the stars and galaxies of heaven faded into the dawn of the sun. It was still early and a little cold, so Lezar rolled closer to Talitha for warmth, and for a few more minutes of easy sleep. With her back to him and with his arms around her in their soft bed, things were good. Both could be comfortable for a little while yet.

Because the evening had been warm, Lezar and Talitha left the window above their bed open for the night breeze. Now, with the colder early morning, both relished the warmth of the blanket. Both considered and rejected sitting up to close the window.

Lezar watched the stars begin to fade in the early morning. As he watched, he wondered just how far it might be to the end of the Lord's creation. Could it be as far through the sky as Damascus of Syria? Or perhaps as far through the sky as Rome was on the ground from Capernaum? Nevertheless, it seemed a long distance from Capernaum to the end of Creation.

Lezar enjoyed these precious minutes of thinking about

the Creation, and about the Lord. He saw himself as something of an expert in these thoughts. On some days, Lezar learned some fantastic new fact about some part of Creation. Then, for the next day or two, he would be unable to sleep with the excitement of new knowledge.

One evening, Lezar realized one light in the sky appeared to get brighter and move more rapidly across the sky. Only the shooting stars moved faster than this light. Then it seemed the light produced a tail shooting out a long, long distance, away from the setting sun. It could not be a shadow, for it was at night. Then, a few mornings later, the tail pointed just the other way, away from the rising sun. Lezar puzzled on this a long while, but could not quite understand its meaning.

Talitha also puzzled over things she could learn about life. Talitha enjoyed learning about her own responsibilities for the little family. One of her personal favorite things was weaving cloth for their clothing. She liked to make cloth from different materials for robes, and tunics. Lezar made the sandals, but Talitha made the rest. She colored some threads in berry or bark or flower dyes to make brightly colored clothes. Somehow, it seemed these clothes made even the days seem a little brighter.

As did most of the men around Capernaum, Lezar fished on the lake frequently. He dried most of the fish he caught on wood racks along the shore. He traded these fish for many things.

He traded for flour, so Talitha could make those little loaves of bread. Then Lezar could dip the loves in berry juice, or in lamb gravy. Or they could put dried fish between halves of a loaf, and eat them.

Sometimes Lezar traded for leather, or for thread, or pitch or tar for the boat. They needed many items to sustain life around the Sea of Galilee.

Lezar and Talitha agreed with each other on the course their lives should take. Both enjoyed learning new facts and details and concepts for their lives. This new goal had to be something which would be central to their marriage. So Lezar and Talitha had a little pact about knowledge and personal growth.

The two lovers agreed that some amazing opportunity might present itself sometime. If it did, they would look for a way to take up the possibility. They would even go so far as to sell their home and their furniture. They would purchase a donkey or a horse or camel if they needed one. They could hit the road with the vision of a new adventure. Preparing for the new life would be so exciting!

Lezar and Talitha even tried to foresee what the new adventure might be. They considered moving to the Decapolis to teach in one of the many Greek schools there. Traveling on the Mediterranean Sea with the

Phoenicians or the Egyptians might be exciting. Signing on with a caravan headed for Macedonia and Rome, or Damascus and China would tempt them. It would be irresistible to a couple who had known only Galilee. So they dreamed of the future, and even prayed for the new life, whatever it might be.

Lezar saw himself as a scholar of people. Capernaum was a great place to study persons from many different ethnic, racial and religious groups. Every day saw caravans from Scandinavia, Gaul, China and every part of Africa stopping for trade or just rest. Lezar watched their customs and listened to their languages. He noticed how each group impacted Capernaum society. Every time, he admired their willingness to keep moving on at the close of their visit.

As days went on, Lezar began to spend more time with the growing group established around the tax collector's tent. This was a fun group, most of the time. Some jokes were a little rough. Some were spoke of times. Men or women might have new problems with a family or a business. If so, the group seemed to always take the matter as seriously as needed.

One man in the group always supported whomever needed his help. Jesus was a carpenter who had arrived just a few months ago from Nazareth. When Jesus arrived in town, he worked for a time as a carpenter. Soon Jesus was spending more time in the portion of the tourism industry which focused on healing.

This healer worked with a varied selection of needy people. Some had problems of their own, such as epilepsy or skin diseases or relationships with family members. Some came to Jesus with family members in trouble. Occasionally the issue was a mental or spiritual disease. Sometimes the problem was a matter of an inability to provide food for children or grandchildren.

Lezar noticed Jesus did not seem selective in any way about those he helped overcome their personal issues. Rich or poor, strong or weak, male or female, old or young; everyone was welcome whenever Jesus operated in a healing mode. He always seemed ready.

Some stranger could come into town crippled, having struggled from Damascus or Sidon. Jesus almost always immediately made time for the target of his healing ministry. Often, the work took only a few seconds of a touch and a few words. More often, Jesus asked someone to be beside him for a little time. Then Jesus carried on a lengthy conversation with the client. Telling stories and demonstrating his talent and his special gifts of the healing arts were Jesus' style.

Lezar frequently voiced his amazement and admiration of this work of Jesus to Talitha. "I really admire the way he works," said Lezar. "Jesus really must have had a great income in Nazareth, before he came here. He seems not to need to work much at all to keep going. He always has the time to just stop his work and deal with whomever comes to him at any point. I do not believe I could keep bringing home enough to support you if I stopped my work that often. I would like to do it, but I am afraid to try. Besides, I guess the opportunity has not come up yet. Maybe I will never know what I would do."

Talitha rubbed Lezar's shoulders for a few moments while she thought about this situation. As she massaged, Talitha looked around at their tidy little home and the few precious artifacts of a good life. Everything seemed too precious to let it go as they searched for the fulfillment of the good life.

"Lezar, you will see Jesus again soon. Perhaps you should ask him about himself. Ask him how he has prepared himself for doing what he does. I am sure he would tell he. He really seems like a man who can tell you about his own work, and dreams. He will answer the call to do what he must do. Maybe he can give you some ideas for your own dreams."

Lezar thought for a moment. "I guess you are right. He is a good man; I know he is. I think he would do anything he could for anyone. Maybe he can help me do the same sort of work. Now, that would be exciting, I think. Perhaps we could find a way to get into something like that. It would probably not be around here, because he has this territory, I guess. I will try to ask him, when I see him again."

A day or two later, Lezar sat in the circle in front of the tax collector's tent. Jesus did not join the group for a couple hours. He might have been healing someone, or even out fishing someplace, or building something for someone. When Jesus appeared, Lezar was ready. Yet still he had to wait until the conversation was quiet again.

His question for Jesus grew inside him through these hours since he talked with Talitha about Jesus and his work. As time went on, Lezar grew more impatient with the burn of his heart and hands.

However, the time to ask came. The ring around Jesus and Lezar was quiet. "Jesus, I have a, uh, well, hypothetical question for you. You know my wife, Talitha, pretty well. She and I have been talking about what we should do with our lives. You know that money is not a big thing with us. We can get by on very little."

"However, we think we might want to, well, do something that is more exciting, more valuable to the world. Just for instance, look at yourself. You just sort of wander around, healing people, making their lives better. We think that is a very good example of the think we would like to do."

"So, Jesus, my question is for you. How did you get

ready to do what you do? What kind of training did you get? Did you go to school someplace? You do not seem to make much money, yet you never are short of anything. Did you have much stuff, a house you built and sold, maybe some nice furniture to sell so you could come to Capernaum and Bethsaida and not have to work hard for a while? I suppose once your work as a healer gets off the ground, it will be all right. It should pay enough that you will not lack for cash or anything else."

"So, Jesus, Talitha and I think that would be good work for us. We think maybe that is what we should do. So what is it we should do to get ready? Is there a school we should attend? How much money do we need to raise to get set up in business as healers and personal helpers?"

Jesus seemed to pause a moment before answering Lezar's question. Levi, the tax collector, had a quick answer for Lezar. "Lezar, my friend, it is good you have happened along today. It is just by coincidence that they authorize me to make you a special deal. I can let you have both Capernaum and Bethsaida Healer Licenses for both you and Talitha. Two for the price of one. That is, you get licenses to heal, both in Capernaum and Bethsaida. Then you can work in either town for only one hundred denarii. Now, where is that quill so I can write it out? I can even write it so it is good in the whole of Galilee! You should be glad you came today."

Now even Jesus laughed at Levi. Everyone laughed. Jesus waited for the laughter and coarse responses to die down before he began to answer Lezar.

When everything, even the whole world, seemed to silently wait for Jesus' words, he began his parable. "Lezar, I think you and Talitha should hear this now. I believe you are ready."

"The kingdom of heaven will be something like this, I believe. Once upon a time, ten bridesmaids prepared for a wedding. They were in a town not too far from here, but a town a lot like Capernaum. They took their lamps and went to meet the bridegroom on the wedding night. Five of the bridesmaids were, well, foolish. Five were wise."

"When the foolish took their lamps, they took no more oil with them. The sharp bridesmaids took extra flasks of oil with their lamps. Everything was ready. Everyone was excited for the fun of the wedding."

"Would you not know what was coming? Of course. They delayed the bridegroom. All the bridesmaids slept while they waited for the bridegroom. Hours went by as they waited."

"At midnight someone shouted, 'Look! The bridegroom has arrived! Come out to meet him!' All the bridesmaids woke up and began to trim their lamps. The foolish girls said to the wise, 'Give us some of your oil, for our lamps are going out.' The wise could only say,

'Sorry. We can not do that. The oil will not be enough for you and for us as well. You should go find a dealer who is open now, and buy some for yourselves.' Now the foolish girls went to buy some oil. While they were gone, the bridegroom arrived. Those who were ready went with him into the wedding banquet. The family closed the door against latecomers."

"Sometime later the foolish bridesmaids returned. 'Lord, Lord, open the door.' He replied, 'I do not know you!'"

"So, Lezar, you have heard the parable. You and Talitha know what to do." Neither Lezar, nor Levi, nor any other, could say anything.

# 43. The Day is Coming
## Luke 9
### The temporary nature of the finest construction.
### Gospel Time: 380

Jesus walked very slowly around the temple. Someone asked if he had seen it before. Many faithful Jews never had an opportunity to stand where Jesus stood now. Many never saw the magnificent building in their lifetime.

As he made his little tour of the reconstructed buildings and walls, Jesus was very quiet. Often he ran his hand over a statue or a large stone, sensing the elaborate beauty of the work.

Jesus knew many stonecutters, carpenters and masons poured out their faithful hearts into the temple through their hands. The carvings, the fittings, the imagery were the finest work they could produce for their Lord. They were willing to produce so much because they believed the Lord gave them so much.

Herod the Great had a great image of the future temple of the Jews. He knew the temple begun by Solomon was the most beautiful building ever constructed. It had massive carved pillars and wall stones the size of small chariots.

Within himself, Herod found himself competing with

Solomon for the hearts and admiration within the Hebrew people. He was not really Hebrew, but Idumean. Herod felt obliged to gain his royal credentials as a legitimate King of the Jews. He could do this by going "over the top" with every royal activity.

When Herod put together an army, it was good. The army was larger and tougher and better trained than any other the nation had ever known. When Herod handed out punishment for a crime, the flogging was more violent than that of any other government. When a trumpet sounded, it had to be louder and stronger and longer than any other.

So now Herod was rebuilding the temple. It would be larger and stronger and more beautiful than ever before. Even yet the workers were placing statuary of cherubim and seraphim on pedestals around the temple. Figures of babies with wings and lions with wings were everywhere. Many decorations covered the massive sacrificial altar on its sides and legs.

Surely Solomon, in all his glory, never saw anything like this. King Saul, who railed against buildings, would have tore his hair out. Just as surely, because of all this strength and beauty, Herod could probably convince the Jews of one thing. He could show he was the legitimate heir and ruler of the nation of Solomon and David, Josiah and Ezekiel. He was the only man alive who could bring this about. He could transform the nation from a tiny Middle Eastern plot to a major world power along the Jordan River.

It would not matter that Herod's family were Edomites. It surely did not matter that Herod's ancestors came from the desert lands across the Jordan. It should matter, even to these people, only that Herod could fulfill his promise. He could build one of the mightiest nations on earth out of an insignificant little has-been of a nation.

Now as Jesus walked around the temple grounds his mood began to change, to grow darker. Often a disciple pointed out to him some outstanding piece of architecture. It was a particularly beautiful piece of wood, carved into some important sign of the faith. Or it was a brilliant sandstone slab, laid in a carefully chosen spot. Its beauty would show forever in the Jerusalem sun.

Jesus watched everything as they walked. He saw that many workers were poor pilgrims from far lands. They were forced into labor when they approached the temple on their journey of faith. He saw men of Asia, and deep Africa, and northern Europe. Some volunteered. Some hired for the pay. Many were not faithful Jews. They were there because the Romans captured them in war. Some hired on with money paid from the treasury of Herod or the temple.

Yes, Jesus was happy to see the temple rebuilt. Yes,

Jesus knew why Herod was rebuilding the temple. Yes, Jesus saw the good that was coming from all this construction. Jesus also saw the evil that lay all around him.

In the middle of the great construction Jesus found himself responding in his heart to the poverty of the street. Old men and women, barely staying alive in their hunger, cried out to every passerby for food. Some pilgrims were carrying caged birds and animals to the altar for sacrifice. They walked right past the starving ones, looking neither to right nor left as they passed.

Almost everyone walking into the newly rebuilt temple courtyard had some kind of treasure with them. A little gold, some silver, diamonds, other jewels. Sometimes just bread or fruit or some other goods for the sacrifice. Everyone who entered carried something. Jesus could not fail to notice.

Only a few offered any of their food to the poor as they passed. Some pilgrims walked quickly past the box for the poor as they moved through the courtyard. Some dropped a coin or two into the box. Whenever this happened, those waiting around only watched and waited. Finally a priest came to gather the coins, then spread the cash among a few special poor. Most would get nothing.

Jesus attracted some attention as he walked around the temple. He touched every stone, every board he could reach. He appeared to try to remember every detail as if he might never see it again. Even little children walked close to him, but left him to experience for himself the beauty of the rebuilding. Some men and women came from the far corners of the courtyard to be a part of the pageant. Yesterday citizens hailed him as King. Today he walked through the blessed temple of the people. Whatever he said and acted on today must be extremely important.

Jesus moved slowly around the temple grounds. He carefully studied both the temple reconstruction and the people in and around the temple. One young mother carried her baby in a sling in front of her. She walked near the gate to the inner courtyard. Then she knelt where she could see the action inside.

As the mother knelt she spread some oil over her baby's hair and face and body. As Jesus watched, she said a few words into the air. Then she kissed her baby on the cheek and spoke softly to the child for a moment. Then, in silence, she closed her eyes and wept. Then, without another word, she looked to the heavens. The beautiful young mother stood, with the child still in the sling, and walked away from the temple. Jesus might have been the only one who saw her go.

You might have seen his lips move in his own simple prayer for mother, and child, and nation.

Jesus walked on around the rebuilding work. As he neared the back of the courtyard, he stood beneath a fig tree. The tree was left over from earlier times, before Herod's reconstruction began. The little shade was a pleasant respite from the broiling sun of Jerusalem.

Now Jesus sat on a stone bench placed there for weary pilgrims. Now, whenever Jesus sat down it might be a signal that he was ready to talk for a while. Someone brought him some fresh water to help clear his voice. Then, as usual, another voice rose with a question.

"Jesus, yesterday you came into the city. Many of us called you king of the Jews. We thought you were going to run Herod out. Today, the court looks as if nothing has changed. Have you missed the time when your words and your actions could have made the big change in the world? Did you miss the time? Or did you not speak strongly enough? I would not complain, you understand. Perhaps I just did not grasp the meaning of the events, or the timing. I just want to know what is happening."

Jesus looked at the questioner easily, smiling. "Do not worry, friend. You did not miss a thing. Let me tell you something. I have been here before. I was born at Bethlehem, just over there. The time was not right just yet. When I turn twelve, my parents brought me to the temple. The rebuilding was not too far along. However, I could see what it would look like when it was finished."

"Then, a couple more times I have come. I have come to serve here as a priest at the altar, as does every priest who can. The time has not been right."

"Look at this fig tree over my head. When you see the first tiny shoots come out on the limbs you say "Spring is here. The time is right. Then, at some time you see the first leaf fall, and you say, 'The time is right.' When the time is right, you will know. Just as you know when the time has come for the leaf to form on the tree, you will know. Just as you know when the time has come for the leaf to fall from the tree, you will know. You will know when the time has come for the Son of Man to find his place among the heavens. You will know."

Another voice rose up. "It sounds as if you are also speaking of the rebuilding of the temple. Are you saying something about the temple?"

Now Jesus was speaking very carefully. "Let me tell you a thing about the temple. One day the temple you see rising again before you will fall down. Every rock, every board, will come loose and crash to the ground. It will take another forty years to rebuild that temple. I am not talking about that temple. I am talking about another temple. They will destroy the temple of which I speak. In three days they will rebuild it, and nothing shall ever dislodge it."

Now, only silence. No person could fail to understand

these words were a challenge to the Herodians. They pushed the Herodians to rebuild the temple of the Jews.

No one had any understanding of the meaning of his words about his body and spirit. No one could understand until three days after he died.

Jesus rested in the silence under the fig tree for a time. He knew destruction was at hand.

"We should go now. It will soon be time for sleeping."

# 44. You Sweet Man
## John 2 and 3
Each person sees Jesus differently.
Gospel Time: 390

Judas could hardly believe his eyes. He knew they were telling the truth. He saw this coming long ago from his overall knowledge of the operation. It was coming, and he could do nothing to stop the catastrophe, it seemed.

This careful bookkeeper was maybe the ultimate micro-manager of all time. That hand wrote the financial detail that kept the disciples fed and sheltered. That brain figured the money needed for Jesus' many trips. That mouth gave the words which encouraged many to contribute to Jesus' upkeep around Capernaum. He was important to the whole future of the world.

Now the group arrived in Jerusalem. Living might be tougher here. As outsiders, finding expense money might be very difficult. The other men were glad to let Judas micro manage their lives.

Judas' work was long and hard. Jesus could always stretch the available food to satisfy the disciples and others around. Shelter was easy. Many Galileans, Samaritans and Judeans offered shelter to the disciples for sleeping. Beds were usually only pallets of straw or a featherbed on the floor of a home. So the disciples could live nicely, thank you.

Today was different. Judas saw this coming long ago. He warned Jesus and some other disciples about this sort of event. they obviously did not listen. Now it would cost the group dearly. Judas was beside himself with frustration and bitterness.

Women. Women were the problem. Well, not really. It was the relationship between a man and a woman. Judas thought every woman wanted to be close to Jesus. Because Jesus usually only talked with people in groups, he was usually safe from a woman's clutches. Often a woman tried to get close to Jesus, but failed. Then her next step was to make a pitch for a disciples. Peter and Philip often attracted these potential trail-snakes. A couple even tried to grab Judas. He assumed they expected the disciples had lots of money, there for the taking by a zealous camp follower.

Marla had a different life. She had her own wealth. Marla was attractive, personality-wise. She wore nice clothing and cared carefully for her own body and soul. Even Judas and the other men watched as she moved among them. Marla moved gently and carefully around the group, making life a little better for all of them. Her long, wavy black hair blew gently in the breeze or bounced with her steps as she worked. Her gentle voice and calm self-awareness made her welcome wherever she moved. Even Jesus seemed glad to have her around. Life was not easy for Jesus and the disciples. The continuing crowd could be a welcome nuisance at times.

Marla came to the group a few days earlier. Already she made her own way among them. Jesus spent some time with a few young families, early in the day. While Jesus and the parents talked, Marla organized a small day care for the children. This gave Jesus some quiet time with the parents. It was good.

At lunch, Marla helped prepare and lay out the dried fish, bread, fruit and wine for those who were near. Now, late in the day, Marla sat near Jesus as he relaxed with the close group. At evening, Jesus preferred to just sit around with the disciples, talking about the events of the day.

Tonight, Marla listened quietly to Jesus for a few minutes. As he talked, her mind drifted off to the love of her life, Galus. Oh, Marla did miss Galus so much. While Galus lived, he traveled often, and for long periods. Sometimes he took his small caravan to India, Egypt or Rome. While her children were growing, Marla seldom traveled with Galus on his longer trade routes. More often, she stayed home, hiring a servant to help her keep her sanity. Her two children were good, but sometimes she just needed a break.

Galus often brought Marla and the children nice toys

and trinkets from exotic places. On a trip to India, when the children were small, he found a beautiful little alabaster vial of nard. It should be for Marla. It was very expensive, but he loved her so much! He worked off the extra time and energy required to make the gift happen. The nard was a year's wage for a middle class family of Judea. Every day looked brighter as Marla remembered the look on Galus' face. As he placed the beautiful alabaster vial of nard in her hand, his eyes kissed her. That look was treasure enough for a lifetime.

Now Galus was gone. He came home for a few months between trading trips. Then the time came to move on. Persia was calling him again, it seemed. Even while he prepared for another long absence, Marla was so happy to have him near. One morning, just before Passover last year, Galus simply did not awaken from his sleep.

It took some time, but Marla eventually could move around with her friends and her family again. The children were grown now, with families of their own. Marla heard Jesus was coming to town. She made a little time to hear what he had to say. She liked it. He helped her feel good about Galus again.

Judas raised again his worrying hand. "Jesus, I really need to talk to you about something. This is so important that you cannot ignore it any longer. We are broke. Skinned. Out of money and nearly out of food. Or anything. What am I supposed to do about that? Tell us all what we must do."

Jesus scowled for a moment, then answered Judas. Well, a little bit of a scowl, anyway. "Judas, I think you are worrying over something that is not going to happen. You are planning for me for a month from now, or a year from now. I think that is not necessary." Jesus went on, talking about his mission and his vision of the future.

As Marla sat near Jesus, she listened as Jesus opened his vision of the possibilities of this world. Marla idly fingered the small vial in her small waist bag. She sometimes carried the precious thick oil with her. With every touch, the oil reminded her of Galus and her children. She felt a comfort and a goodness from his presence with the oil in her little bag.

Marla moved behind Jesus, kneeling behind him. With a gentle touch, Marla began to straighten Jesus' hair with her ivory comb. Jesus smiled a little, obviously enjoying this little service. This had been a long day, and her attention gave him some peace.

While she knelt there, she took the nard from her bag. Marla gazed silently at the vial for a few moments, remembering the good times before Galus died. She fingered the artwork on the tiny bottle, seeing only his eyes as he placed the vial in her hands. Then, holding the fragile piece in the palm of her hand, she broke it open with a small rock. The thick oil poured out into her palm.

With her other hand, Marla carefully divided the precious oil into several small portions. One portion found its way into Jesus' hair. She spread the oil around gently with one hand. A second portion went to the back of his neck. It soothed the skin, hard and coarse from years of walking and working in the sun.

Marla gathered a few drops in her hand. She spread it on the brow and cheekbones of a small girl in her mother's arms.

Marla made a move toward Judas as he sat near Jesus. Judas blocked her with his hands as he began his protest. He was almost speechless, but not quite.

So Marla turned back to Jesus. She took the remaining few drops of oil in her hands and rubbed it on his face. Jesus seemed to enjoy the act of tenderness. He smiled and simply let Marla continue her task as he talked and listened.

Marla finished working the nard oil into Jesus' cracked and weathered face and hands. Then she reached out to spread a little oil on his ears and neck. She gently worked the oil into his dry and brittle skin. Then she pulled his head toward her to give him a little hug.

Marla's face rested gently against his cheek for a brief moment, as often happens with a hug. She began to pull away, but in the movement, her lips touched his for a moment, and quickly moved on. For just that moment, the beauty of Marla's relationship with Galus came back again. The sensation of his presence in the touch of Jesus filled her with the old sense of love and care. Galus was so good, and their love was everything a husband and wife could want. It just did not last long enough. Remembering was good, if only for a moment. Just a little embarrassed now, Marla mumbled "I'm sorry."

Jesus pulled Marla to him again, holding her against his shoulder. After a moment, Marla again sat next to Jesus. Tears filled her eyes, and her heart overflowed with the vision of her beloved Galus, alive again for her.

As Marla sat down again, Judas could hold his tongue no longer. "Jesus! Listen to me! You are not thinking clearly! That nard oil she just spread all over you, and on that baby, was worth a fortune. We have not had that much money between us since you called us all together! They could have sold that ointment and the vial itself, and we could have given half to the poor, and still have had more than we have ever had together. Good grief! We could have given it all to the poor!?"

"Do you not care, Jesus? Are you blind to yourself, and what you mean to all these poor people who have no hope? Come on, Jesus. Get with it!"

Suddenly the disciples and the others were silent. No one ever spoke this way to Jesus, at least not in front of others. Jesus waited a bit, then responded. His voice was almost too gentle as he began.

"Judas, I know you worry about what is happening. You do not need to worry. You will always have the poor with you. You can give them something anytime. You will not always have me with you. When I am gone, you can give the poor everything you have. In truth, that is what you must do."

"Marla has done a beautiful thing for me with this gift from Galus, her husband. He gave this beautiful gift to her to use for anything that makes her happy. She has opened the vial now. The perfume of that oil of love will stay with her forever. Every time she catches a whiff of that beautiful flowery scent, she will remember Galus. Every time she thinks of me, she will remember good things of her Lord. What more could she ask of the Lord's creation?"

"Marla has done a beautiful thing for me. She has used me as a way to remember the goodness of her husband. She could remember his love for her, and her love for him. She will also remember my love for her, and her love for me. Now, let us have no more grumbling about those who do good to me. Judas, I believe you have work to do."

Judas drifted to the outskirts of the group of disciples. Turning his back to Jesus, Judas walked away toward the temple. He had plans. His plans were to fill the treasury of the small group of disciples. Surely, an intelligent man like Judas could find a way to sweet-talk some dumb priests out some money. He might even get enough cash to rebuild the treasury for Jesus and the disciples. It would not take much to see them back to Galilee; just a few silver or gold coins.

# 45. One Persistent Woman
Luke 18:1-8; Psalm 143; 147:12-20;
Deut. 16:18-20, 17:14-20; 2 Cor. 8:1-16
Strength in the heart.
Gospel Time: 400

Paula wrapped her feet more tightly in the blanket. The cold night air ate into her bones as she lay on the straw mattress in the old shelter.

At the time the shelter was just a barn and a workshop. Two or three boats in various stages of construction were usually kept in the old building. Paula and Reuben kept a few animals in the barn at night. A couple cows, a donkey, a few sheep and several chickens. Then, during the day, they chased the animals out to make room for their boat business.

This business was not much, as estates went. It was barely enough to keep a husband and wife going. Reuben was getting on in years. He had worked hard all his life, building and repairing boats for the fishermen who scoured the Sea of Galilee.

Reuben and Paula did all right, working together. Their little home was comfortable for the two of them. They had no children, so they had few visitors into their home. Once they thought they were pregnant, but something went wrong. Paula had bled for a few days. After that, she had no signs of pregnancy.

Later in life, things began to change in their lives. Reuben's hands began to shake as he worked. He finally could no longer do the fine work on his boats. More and more each day he relied on Paula to spread the pitch and tar on the fishing boat. Then Reuben's voice began to waver. Paula had to do more and more of the bargaining for the price of the boats.

When this happened, some customers began to try to take some advantage of her. Some of them even said that, because she was a woman, Paula could not understand boats. She could not understand their bigotry, but she knew it was real.

At these times Paula prayed a lot. She asked the Lord to protect her from people who tried to hurt Reuben and Paula. She even began to ask the people around the community to help shield Paula and Reuben from these people. These potential customers acted like thieves.

Most of their old customers honored their long relationships with the boat-builders of Capernaum. If they needed a boat, they went to Paula. They made the same deal s they had made for many years. If they needed repairs, they knew Paula and Reuben could do just as well now. Her skill was as great as that of two together before Reuben took on his Parkinson's. Their money now was just as good as it had been for many years.

Reuben still did most of the harder work on the boats. Although his society did not yet know the name, Reuben had a growing affliction of Parkinson's Disease. Reuben and Paula only knew he could no longer work as he once did.

Paula had to work a little harder each day to keep things going. In just a few years, Reuben's Parkinson's developed to the point he had difficulty even taking care of himself. This forced Paula to double up on her work again. She now had to take care of Reuben and also sell and build the boats and repair them.

Even this she could do. She learned to work quickly and efficiently. Paula slept only a few hours now at night. Her muscles ached from working with the boats, and working with Reuben. She kept up her little production line, but each boat took a little longer than the one before.

The one thing she could do now just as beautifully as before was pray. Each morning, before the sun came up, just as dawn began to appear over Bethsaida, Paula prayed. Sometimes she prayed one of the old Psalms of David. Sometimes she remembered a few words of Amos, or Ezekiel. Sometimes she spoke to the Lord from her own heart.

She had so many words to say to the Lord. She talked to the Lord about her worry over Reuben. She spoke of her own frustrations of more and more work in the face of Reuben's Parkinson's Disease. On some days, Paula could only pray silently. She prayed for the people who tried to cheat her in an agreement to build a boat.

On these days, she could not bring herself to speak aloud the names of those who attempt to wrong her. She could, however, remember some of David's Psalms or the condemnations of Amos. Remembering the soothing promises of Isaiah was most difficult. She worried about her own standing before the Lord when she voiced those evil thoughts about her own enemies. Nevertheless, life went on.

In the evening, Paula's prayers were very simple. She gave thanks to the Lord that she survived another day. She promised the Lord she would try to do better tomorrow. That was about it. Day after day, morning and evening.

Then came the day of the great disaster. Paula could not awaken Reuben. Usually, she had her morning bath, then prepared a little breakfast of some bread. Perhaps she had some fruit or nuts, and even a dried fish. When everything was ready, Reuben was awake and ready to take his tiny meal. Then Paula helped him eat, and gave him a morning bath.

Not today. On this morning, Reuben did not move. Paula knew for a long time that this day would come. She thought she was ready for the hard time it would bring. She sat down beside Reuben where he lay silently. She kissed his still lips, now cooling in the cool morning air. Running her hands over his face, she pulled his eyelids shut, and pressed his mouth closed.

Now Paula went next door for help. Ondie and Mary Elizabeth were good neighbors. Often they helped Paula with Reuben when she could not handle his needs alone. Ondie immediately went to find the rabbi and some other helpers to bury Reuben.

Mary Elizabeth asked Ondie to send some women to help her and Paula to prepare Reuben for burial. The people who came that morning were friends and customers of Reuben and Paula for many years. The men went immediately dug a grave in the burial plot on the dry sand dune just away from town. Then they returned to the home.

The women rubbed some olive oil into Reuben's skin. Then they wrapped Reuben in clean cloths. When the rabbi came, and spoke the prayers of death and burial, they were ready. The rabbi led the way to the grave. Then came the men, carrying Reuben on a sheet, strung between the ends of a pole. Then Paula, with some friends.

When Reuben was safely in the ground, Paula and some other women sat nearby. They used this time to talk about Reuben's life. He was a good man, and a good provider. Only when Parkinson's invaded his life did he fail to provide for Paula.

The men left the grave to return to Capernaum. Finding Jesus now seemed the normal thing to do. They expected Jesus to be at the tax collector's tent. This was the gathering place for several of his friends in the morning. They men sat or stood and talked about all the affairs of the day.

Today, as they came near the tent, someone asked where the men had been in the early morning. They replied they had been to help Paula bury Reuben. Everyone knew Reuben. When he could, he was a frequent visitor to the Tent Flap Group at the tax collector's tent.

One man, a long-time customer of Reuben and Paula, spoke openly. "Well, now perhaps she can get on with building the boats she has promised. She promised me a boat three months ago, and she has still not made it ready. Now, perhaps she can. Or will."

The little group sat in stunned silence now. No one expected this rudeness now. Some of them glanced at Jesus to see what he would say. For a moment, Jesus only drew little figures in the dust with a stick.

Then Jesus spoke quietly. "I have heard her prayers."

Again, silence while the others contemplated Jesus'

words in the hush of the moment.

"Once upon a time, in a town not too far away, many prayers sounded in the synagogue. A judge who had no fear of the Lord nor any respect for the people held court. He was not a good man to serve as a judge."

Now, in that city, lived a widow who required his help. He would not help her. He believed such cases were below him. The widow was persistent, however. She told the judge she needed justice against her troubler. Since he was the one who could help her, she needed his help now.

For a time the judge refused to help. He would not have anything to do with this poor woman. Then he changed his mind. He thought, 'I don't care about the Lord. I do not respect any person but myself, yet I must do something. Because this woman deeps bothering me, I will give her what she asks for. If I do not, she may wear me out by continually coming to me.'

Jesus paused, then went on. "Such is the Kingdom of Heaven."

Jesus again began to draw figures in the dust with a stick. The man who complained about Paula sat quietly now, his head down. The other men also were quiet. No one had any question of the meaning of the parable.

# 46. Homecoming
## Luke 6:20-49
### Jesus visits his parish.
### Gospel Time: 405

As Jesus left Chorazin on the road to Capernaum, he felt the fatigue in his bones. The road would be hot on his feet today. It should become cooler as he neared the Sea of Galilee. The sun should be cooler, but it would not be. He knew the dust would get warmer as he moved down to the water, about six hundred feet below sea level. At this elevation the sun throws angry rays at the volcanic dust of the road.

The heat began to work its way into his bones as he walked with his people. Little rivulets of dust ran ahead of his feet with each step. They pointed the way ahead as he walked.

Each rut in the main highway between Chorazin and Capernaum served as a channel for the rivers of dust. This was a major road northwest of Lake Tiberias, between the lake and the mountain resorts. Thousands of years of travelers ground the path into a powder. Even the few centuries of Akkadian, Greek, Roman and Egyptian armies created problems. Moving through this territory ground even more roadway into dust.

On this trip, Jesus walked along many miles of ancient

road to carry his ministry to far communities. Tiberias, Nazareth, Tyre, Sidon, Chorazin and a hundred villages and settlements between them. At each stop, eager people came from miles around to hear and to be healed. Jesus felt himself rested and renewed by the great reception he received almost every day.

When Jesus came to Nazareth, things did not go as he hoped. Jesus came into Nazareth two evenings before the sabbath. He taught and healed in his home town through the next day. Some of his old friends came around to talk about some good old times.

When Jesus began to talk about the temple and his call for temple righteousness, a few of those sitting around began to whisper among themselves. Later, Jesus noticed these same few men left the gathering before he finished for the day.

On the sabbath, Jesus went early to the synagogue. He entered, then sat in prayer for several minutes. As the custom was, the rabbi asked him to choose one of scrolls to read to the congregation. After reading, a visitor such as Jesus should expect to explain his understanding of the words of the scroll.

Jesus took down one of the scrolls of Isaiah and began to teach. His demand for righteousness and his promise of healing should have been most welcome. After all, this was his home town, the town where his father risked his life as a young man. Joseph found the strength to resist the tyranny of Herod and Rome night after night.

This morning, however, Jesus was not welcome in the synagogue at Nazareth. His words were surely a battle cry aimed at the Herodians and the Romans in Jerusalem. At part way through the talk, one man Jesus thought he knew rose and left the synagogue. Jesus could not be sure, but he thought this man was someone Joseph knew years ago in Nazareth. However, today he left before Jesus could learn his identity.

As Jesus ended his teaching, several men left the room. Jesus appeared to understand their mission. As he left the building, the men and some of the women began to shout at him. They threw clods of dirt at him as if to drive him away from their down.

Jesus understood their anger. The people of his home town were afraid of the Herodians and the Romans. If either of these tyrannical groups learn of Jesus' harsh words today, either might come to Nazareth. They could and would destroy the town, the homes, the synagogue, the tents in just a few minutes. They might even kill many of the residents. So they tried to at least make a show that they did not agree with Jesus' words.

Jesus only shielded himself from their attacks. He quoted on of the scrolls to them. "A prophet is not without honor except in his own town." On the day after the sabbath, Jesus left for the coastal towns.

Now, months later, Jesus was headed home. His last major stop, Chorazin, served as almost a victory party. Hundreds turned out for this final showcase of healing and demand for temple righteousness.

Now even that stop was history. Only a few settlements along the road to Capernaum called him to stop for a time of rest, food and water. Then he would be back home. These were great days to be alive.

Jesus probably had a sense of what was coming as he walked closer to Capernaum. If he did see it coming, though, he did not make it known to those who walked with him.

As Jesus entered Chorazin three days earlier, he called Joses to himself. "Joses, my brother, please go to Capernaum for me. Tell my friends I will be there in about four days, coming from Chorazin. When we get to Capernaum, we will have a feast to celebrate the homecoming. Then I will tell everyone what I have seen along the way."

"Now go along. Go kiss your wife and children. Tell them I am sorry you had to be gone so long, but you will be home for a time. I will see you in Capernaum."

Capernaum was a great experience for Jesus. Throughout this mission journey, Jesus honed his mission and presentation skills. He practiced making crowds of dozens and hundreds of curious hear his words. He watched the faces of men, women and children as he touched their ailing bodies with his healing hands. Knowing his impact on their lives was critically important to Jesus.

Most especially, Jesus paid attention to his own parables, his own words. One story might have a stronger impact than another on a certain group of listeners. If it did, Jesus might use it more frequently in a similar situation.

Wherever Jesus went, he found something to learn. Always, his goal was the same. The kingdom of heaven was the goal and the mission. To reach the kingdom, his work called him to focus on two pieces. He was to heal those who were broken, and lead the nation, especially the leaders of the temple organization, to utter righteousness.

Healing and righteousness. Righteousness and healing. These demanded every moment of Jesus' work and travel. At one moment he might be answering a cry for healing by some forlorn Galilean. As he worked, he might have his attention called to some unethical social practice among the people. He often found it difficult to serve both causes with a single touch and a few words.

Occasionally Jesus succeeded merging the two missions. His common practice was to touch an epileptic with his healing hands. Then he made the point of the immense personal value of the leper by asking him to appear to a priest as clean. The priest, the leper and everyone who saw this had to admit his point. Jesus saw even the lowest persons as worthy of his mission. The word went around that Jesus cared for the people even more than did the priests, rabbis and chief laity.

So as Jesus walked the last few miles to Capernaum, he saw a crowd waiting for him. On a flat field, near a stream, they waited quietly for their hero to approach. Jesus saw them from a long way off. He smiled to himself.

The pressure was intense. They wanted him to show some greater healing powers. He was gone several weeks. That certainly was long enough to develop some new and fantastic methods of healing. No more mud in the eye. No more washing in the pool at Bethsaida. Make use of some attention-grabbing action.

But new Jesus had another piece of his mission ready. He could speak about a way for the people to respond to the kingdom of heaven. When Jesus reached the crowd on the flat plain, he found a rock. He waited for the people to quiet down, and began.

Jesus used the occasion to make a summary of his mission trip. Each stop along the way began with healings of local people. Healing was the loud cry as Jesus approached any crowd along the way. Perhaps this person could be made to walk straight. That person might have some demon chased away. Sometimes it seemed every Galilean was crippled in some way.

When Jesus finished his healing work, his teaching turned to ethical righteousness based on faith. Some called his theme "temple righteousness." His theme was the same today as it was when he first left Nazareth several years ago. In his early teens, Jesus learned that core message of the faith of Israel by listening to Joseph at the synagogue. He also listened carefully at home while Mary and Joseph talked. Sometimes, while Jesus, Joseph, and the other boys worked together, Joseph told the boys about Israel. He described the national vision and its vision of life and the Lord.

Jesus talked to the crowd in Chorazin about relationships with other persons. He said that living the righteous and graceful life would always make relationships with others best. His acceptance of others was not a matter of weakness, but of affirming grace.

Now, as Jesus finished his mission trek, he held the vision of Joseph before him. Those familiar words from Nazareth of righteousness, faith and relationships gave the power to his own sermon outside Capernaum.

Jesus knew some of the crowd were hungry. He told the disciples to prepare the meal for the small crowd. By now, his people were accustomed to this. Jesus often asked them to prepare a meal for those who happened to be around. Usually, only a very little food was available. Somehow, though, even this small amount was enough. Sometimes it was a loaf or two of bread, or a fish and some figs or other fruit.

The disciples said the usual traditional blessing. Even as they finished passing around the food, one man seemed to be moving closer to Jesus. He apparently wanted a few words with the teacher.

"Sir, a word."

Even before looking up, Jesus answered. "Yes, my friend. What can I do for you?"

After a moment of silence, Jesus did look up. He looked straight into the eyes of the same man he recognized from Nazareth. Without showing recognition, Jesus looked at the much older man. Now he was sure this was that Nazarene.

"Jesus, your father would be proud of you. He often said the same words as we walked together. Joseph talked about the nation, and about the temple. They were very important to Joseph,, to me and to the rest of the Pigs. He must have taught you well."

The man paused again for a moment. "Jesus, did Joseph ever mention someone called 'Hippo' to you? Did he ever talk about the Pigs?"

Jesus thought back to those years. He recalled quiet conversations with Joseph. "Yes, he did, a few times, but not much. But I knew what he talked about. Sometimes as we walked along, traveling to Jerusalem, or to Kinnaret, the Sea of Galilee. He loved Hippo very much. He told me about walking with Hippo. Hippo was strong as a horse. Hippo had a faith and a commitment which were very strong. He was committed to the Lord's temple."

Again, the men paused. "Jesus, I am Hippo. I may not be quite as strong as Joseph told you. I just tried to do what I believed was right. Now I must go. Tell Mary 'Hello' for me and the other Pigs. She will understand. I hope you understand how much the nation and the temple owe to Joseph and the other Pigs." Hippo smiled at Jesus. Then he slowly moved off without another word.

As Jesus stood to make a few more steps toward Capernaum, he looked again at Joseph's old friend, crippled with age. Hippo gave Jesus new reason to be proud of Joseph.

Ahead lay Capernaum and the nation, Israel. Israel and its temple, the lamb of the eye of the Lord. The cool waters of Kinnesaret would be as refreshing to Jesus' feet as the waters of the healing pool of Bethsaida.

The dust of the road made its little streams along the wheel ruts as Jesus walked toward his new life.

# 47. One Man's Vision
## Luke 9:51
## Jesus Leaves Capernaum for Jerusalem
## Gospel Time: 410

Some days are longer than others. The sun now rising over the low hills along the Damascus - Capernaum road promised such a long day. Eli knew this would be a long, long day of heat and struggle. Eli thanked the Lord this was not a day to move his caravan along any distance. Eli knew a long distance day should have started four or five hours ago.

He would have roused his servants with the first dimming of the stars in coming sunlight. One of them prepared a quick meal for Eli and his wife, plus the three other caravan servants. A small piece of bread and some fresh fish he took from North Jordan river in the early light. A handful of berries from the bushes along the river. Some hot mint tea with camel's milk.

When the others finished reloading the camels and horses with their packs, they came in close around breakfast to eat. As they finished, the servants took the camels to the water's edge for one last drink. Then they lined the camels up for the day's journey.

Eli and Conda took their horses into the middle of the

caravan. Two of the servants rode camels and led three camels each at the front of the caravan. Two servants rode at the back with their camels. Eli's little caravan covered thousands of miles in this fashion.

The four servants Eli had with him were a solid group. One of them, Chronos, served Eli for many years. He was the grizzled old veteran of the caravan routes. Eli trusted Chronos completely as they moved around the Mediterranean. Sometimes he even left Chronos in charge of moving the caravan a few miles to another spot. Eli and Conda used the time to visit some relative or tourist attraction along the way.

The other three men were young, probably teenagers. They did the muscle work with the caravan, prepared the meals, and helped guide and protect the caravan. They were a little rowdy sometimes, but Eli liked them a lot. Eli enjoyed having them along.

Eli spent much time with the young men, teaching them his skills in trading and in camel and horse work. They could usually move a long distance before they tired out.

Not today. Eli had no intention of going far. Capernaum was just a half day's journey along the Damascus road. This portion of the road was easy and wide. It followed the North Jordan River southward, right into the heart of Capernaum. Everyone could consider this a day of rest.

Eli was just enjoying his pot of tea as the stranger walked into the camp. Eli knew instantly what the man wished for. He introduced himself as Osan, a Korahite, a Son of Korah. Then he asked for a bit of bread to eat with berries. He picked the berries from bushes along the river.

Eli motion to Chronos, the old-timer among the servants. Chronos pulled out a small loaf he had just packed away, and handed it to the stranger. The man gently and carefully told Eli and Chronos of his gratitude for the gift. Then he began telling his story and his mission.

"I am looking for truth of the history of the Jews. I am looking for righteousness, especially in the temple in Jerusalem. From the days of Moses and Aaron, my people have lived in these hills. Father Korah challenged Moses and Aaron to tell the truth, and to adopt righteousness as a standard. They killed Father Korah. They killed the hundreds who were with Korah."

"So the rest of my family escaped into these hills along the Damascus Road where we have lived ever since. After one thousand years we are still demanding righteousness. Every follower of Moses and Aaron and Saul and David and Josiah owes that to the Creator."

"Now we know temple righteousness is not enough to satisfy our Lord. It is not enough to slaughter the

Passover Lamb just so. It is not enough to burn the proper number of doves on the altar. It is not enough to allow only certain persons to come before the Lord. It is not enough to say meaningless words before the altar of the Most Holy. If you say them while you burn the homes of the poor, it is a double sin. Righteousness is every day, in every thought, in every action."

Eli found himself agreeing deeply with Osan. Eli often felt these same urges as he traveled the roads from Morocco and Gaul to Persia. Eli saw much sin, much cruelty built around religious practices. Eli saw priests of many religions rob and steal and enslave and kill in the guise of following some religious decree or another.

Riding in a caravan for days at a time gives a person time to think about many things. Often Eli rode up alongside Chronos. The two held strong conversations about many ideas they saw in their travels. It made the time pass, and helped both to keep their sanity in the hot sun.

Eli had heard of these strange men, the Sons of Korah, living in the Galilean hills. They followed many stronger voices of the prophets. Amos might be the strongest voice even yet, although he lived seven hundred years earlier. Josiah, and Isaiah, and others lifted their voices. Many years passed since Ezekiel guided the Jews through captivity in Babylon. Everyone wondered, would there be another?

Eli spoke. "Osan, honored sir, I have heard of the Sons of Korah. I know that what you are searching for is an honorable and just thing. Do you have a new voice? Do you have a new echo of thunder in the wilderness to lead your people and the rest of us?"

"Osan, I have heard the sages say the Lord will provide a new messiah to the Jews. I have heard this new messiah will lead us all to righteousness. I believe this is possible, but I also know it will be very dangerous. If the new messiah challenges the unrighteousness of the temple, he will be in danger of his life. The powerful priests can not allow him to speak candidly about the evils of the temple. So what will happen? How will we know this new messiah?"

Osan thought deeply a few moments. "Eli, my new friend, I will tell you what I have heard. I do not know this is true, but I have heard it is. If it is true, it will shake all of Creation. If it is not true, many will lose in the name of this man."

Osan paused a moment, then continued. "You are going to Capernaum, are you not? You will stay there a few days. You will buy and sell and trade and watch what happens. You will meet people. Some of them will be folks you have met before, either in Capernaum or in your travels someplace. Perhaps you have known them in

Damascus, or in Alexandria."

"Many come to Bethsaida and Capernaum for healing. Some come to be cleansed of leprosy. Some are blind, and want to see. I know I would. Some make the journey to heal other serious diseases within the mind, or within the body. They come because they trust the healing power of the Lord."

Now Osan was getting warmed up to his subject, ready to make his point. "After the Lord heals every person, the priest must now declare them clean. A priest must look them over to see if they are clean. If they were blind, can they now see? If they were deaf, can they now hear? So the priest must now certify the healing, else others will not believe."

"Worse than that, the priest must certify that the Lord has healed persons. If he does not, no more diseased tourists will come to Capernaum and Bethsaida. They will not come to spend their money in the city. They will not pay money to the priests around the pool at Bethsaida. That would be bad."

"You know, of course, when the Lord heals you and declared clean, you owe it to the Lord. You must give some money to the priest who declares you healed and clean. You must always give all you can, so the priests try very hard to bring the wealthiest travelers to town."

Again, Osan paused to let his words stew in the ears

and hearts of Eli and his people. "Now, trouble is coming. I can smell it. All the Sons and Daughters of Korah know what is happening in Capernaum."

"A man is rising up. His name in Aramaic is Jesus. It is a name like Joshua, meaning 'he will save the people.' Anyway, Jesus has come up from Nazareth. His father was a carpenter. They say he was born in Bethlehem, the city of David. They also say his mother was a virgin when he was born. It do not know if this is true, but it might be. I do know he has brothers and a sister."

"Now, Jesus is an interesting fellow. First, he is a carpenter and, apparently, a fisherman. He has gathered a group of men around him, and many of them fish Lake Tiberias. They seem to do pretty well. Some have seen them bring in so many fish it might swamp their boats."

"Now, more, and more to the point. The evidence is this Jesus is a healer. We have reports that he has healed. Even some of our own people report their own healing at his touch. The blind see. The deaf hear. Much more."

"The problem is that some of these don't see the need to report to the priests. They do not feel it necessary to certified others as clean. They obviously do not pay the priests to certify them as clean. That is the biggest problem."

Now Osan paused again. He let Eli and Chronos stew on the implications to this turn of events in Bethsaida and

Capernaum. They could immediately see how the priests might take offense at this Jesus. Osan finished his little discourse. "You see, you are going to Capernaum. I hope you will take the time to go find this man. See what he is doing. Look at all those people who are around him. What are they up to? Are they a threat to the temple? Is Jesus going to be able to purify the temple?"

"I need to know if I can believe he has the power. If he is to bring purity to the temple, he must be a powerful man. He might even be godlike, but I do not know. I do know if he tries to purify the temple, he is in just as much danger as Korah. When Korah faced Moses and Aaron, he knew his life was in danger. Perhaps you should warn him, and the people around him. May the Lord, blessed be he, be gracious to you and yours."

Now Osan was finished. He gathered the last few crumbs of bread and tossed them in his mouth. A couple small pieces fell out into his gray whiskers where they were immediately lost. He stood slowly while Eli and Chronos and the others silently rose together. They Osan was gone, back into the hills of Northern Galilee, back to his contemplation on righteousness and purity.

In a few minutes the caravan began moving south. In two or three hours the caravan found its usual resting place. They always set their tents in the market place near the mouth of the North Jordan River. The younger men began to set up tents for a lengthy stay. As they worked, Eli and Chronos walked around the market place together. There, the men agreed they were in a good spot to display their wares to passers-by.

As the men worked, Eli became aware of a small group of men close by. They sat around under a tent awning flap a few yards away. The men seemed to come and go on an irregular schedule, easily and quietly. Some stayed quite a while. Others stayed only briefly.

Eli knew some of them. He especially know the owner of the tent, a tax collector of Capernaum. Eli would have to deal with this fellow soon. That was all right. Paying the tax was a pretty simple means of gaining some security from thieves and other government pests.

In the center of the group was a fellow Eli did not recognize. The others were very comfortable with his presence. Eli thought he might have a chance to meet this man again.

Three or four of the men at the group rose and came over to Eli's camp. They spoke casually to Eli and Chronos. While they chatted, each looked carefully at the wares the young men brought out. The trading goods placed around on rugs on the ground in front of their camp. Eli watched their eyes carefully, noting which leather or silver or gold pieces commanded their attention. While trading, knowing which articles hold the most interest for the buyer is important.

After a time, Eli asked one of his old friends about this Jesus, or Yeshua, or whatever his name was. He said it was not clear to him from Osan what name to use. He just expected someone would know the supposed healer.

The friend laughed. "Oh, sure, we all know him. He is sitting right there." The friend pointed to the man in the center of the tent flap group, laughing and chatting with the others. "That is Jesus. He is a good man. Everyone thinks he's pretty good."

Another man spoke. "Everyone except the priests, of course. They do not like him at all. They say they cannot make money with him around healing people. So, I guess the priests will force him to leave town, if they are able."

Eli entered the conversation. "I am sure they will try. They will destroy him if they can." Then Eli related the comments from Osan about Jesus, about the danger of forcing righteousness on the priesthood. Osan recalled how Moses and Aaron had Korah and his family wiped out. Korah just pushed too hard for righteousness and justice. Eli quoted Osan, "They will destroy him if they can figure out how."

Another friend spoke. "Well, they should get a move on. I hear he is leaving for Jerusalem in a day or two. He has not said what he will do there. I would bet he will take a stab at cleaning up the mess at the temple. He has to clean it up. That is the sort of person he is. That should make everyone happy."

The first spoke again. "Sure it will. That will make everyone happy. Just as you are happy when your wife tells you to go fix the wall or the roof. Grumble, grumble." Everyone laughed.

Later in the evening Eli sat next to Jesus as the cool air began to bring relief. The market and trading camps were ready for tomorrow now. It was a quiet time, a time for reflection and for closeness. Eli knew this might be his only chance to talk with Jesus.

"Jesus, I hear you might be leaving for Jerusalem soon."

"Yes, Eli, that is true. We will leave either tomorrow or the day after."

"Jesus, I need to warn you about something. I know you. If you go into the temple there, you are in trouble. You will stir things up as you have been doing here. The priests and Herod's people will not like it a bit. They are sure to try to stop you."

Jesus only smiled. "Yes, Eli, I suppose they will. I expect them to try something."

"Jesus, you are playing with the big boys now. They can do something bad to you. They might even kill you. Have you thought about that?"

"Yes, Eli, I have. I know what I am doing is dangerous

to them. So, I just have to take what comes. I must say things and I must do things."

So it was. Jesus left in the morning with some others. Eli never saw him again. Alive. As Eli rode into Jerusalem a few months later, he saw three bodies hanging from crosses on a distant hill. Little could he know the truth of the words of Osan. and of his own words.

Amen.

# 48. Lazarus
John 11:1 - 45; Psalm 130;
Ezekiel 37:1-14; Romans 8:6-11
A friend of Jesus dies. Just before Easter
Gospel Time: 420

Jesus had many friends. Many who, whether or not they believed he was the Messiah, just liked the guy. They just cared about him for the person he was.

Among these friends was Lazarus, brother of Mary and Martha. Sometimes Lazarus found Jesus just to tell him some bad jokes. Not dirty, not degrading to anyone. Just awful jokes. Often Jesus laughed and tried to tell some of his own. Jesus was not too good at comedy. Well, unless he was making fun of pharisees or priests or governors. Even then he used comedy to make a point about the new world.

So Jesus enjoyed Lazarus. Their time together was warm and good. As happens to many people, Lazarus became ill suddenly and died a few days later. The family sent for Jesus when Lazarus became ill. However, Jesus did not return to their home immediately.

When Lazarus finally died, everyone around him had their own comments to make. Some spoke openly, some only spoke to themselves in quiet contemplation. Some spoke to the Lord.

Few people look forward to death. Everyone seems to feel the need to say something about death when it comes close. When family or friend knows the nearness of death, talking seems to help.

Jared, a boyhood friend and neighbor, was first to arrive. He came early to see Mary and Martha, the sisters of Lazarus. In the sadness of their crying, Jared tried to give them comfort.

He hugged them both, and they talked about Lazarus. Jared said how Lazarus had been a good friend. He said it must just have been Lazarus' time to die. It must have been the will of the Lord. Yes, that's it. He died because the Lord wanted him to die.

Now another friend, even closer to Lazarus, just about fell apart at Lazarus' death. Lazarus worked with him as a counselor. In their relationship, Lazarus helped him understand and cope with his own problems.

Now with Lazarus gone, he had no friend, no counselor, no one to turn to. The lonely Jared could only sit and sob. Lazarus' death might as well have been his own. The death of one was a total loss for the other.

In those days the nation was in the hands of the Roman army. Roman troops could find shelter wherever they chose in every city and town in Palestine.

The sound of wailing came from a small house. The

squad of Roman soldiers walked by, but the cry did not change. By the sound and the black-draped doorpost, they knew death had visited.

These were men who faced death every day. Their end might come from a street battle, or from training. They might feel the sword in a pitched battle or a hit and run skirmish. Roman attempts to take over another nation usually met bitter guerilla action. Then young men died. As with most armies, no one talked to the soldiers about their own death.

They talked as they walked by. "I do not think anyone will make that much fuss about me when I die."

"What you should do is to marry some really homely woman. Then when you die, she will be in such a sad state! She'll bawl like a sick calf because no one else will ever want her."

"Naaawww. He's too ugly himself. No woman who is desperate enough to want him! When he was born the midwife slapped his mother."

"I do not see why these Jews make so much fuss over anyone. Death really does not mean anything."

"I've killed a hundred or two, and they were all the same. One of these days someone else will kill me. The world will keep on keeping on."

"So what if another dies, especially just another Jew. I do not trust something about these people."

"You know that Jews are so lazy! When one of them dies it is usually three days before anyone notices."

"I think this family is one of those that followed Jesus, the Galilean. Listen! He talks a lot about getting to heaven. Maybe this fellow had his own way and got to leave early."

Inside the house, things were not that calm. Mary and Martha were living through the stages in their mourning. They saw Jesus was to blame for the whole thing. They had sent for him, but he did not come before Lazarus' life was over.

When Jesus came to the door, he was not a friend. The family met him with resentment and self-pity. The cold emotional overtones of personal blame were startling to Jesus.

Mary was the outspoken one. "Jesus, I really thought you cared. All these months you have been telling us how you loved us. You have been saying we should love each other. We believed you."

"You even told us what we should do if we love each other. You said we should do as you do. We have seen you make the blind see. We have seen you make the deaf hear and the epileptic straight."

"What about us? Why do you spend all your time with those people? They will not even walk with you. Why do you care only about some sinners who just do not care about you?"

"Yet you let Lazarus, a man you say you love, just lay down and die. You do not even bother come around until after he is dead. He has even been gone long enough to start smelling bad. Is it asking too much for you to be here when someone is sick? Can you come when someone who loves you is about to die?"

Now it was Martha who spoke. The fire and discouragement in her voice betrayed her sorrow.

"Jesus, I really do not think you care. Maybe you have a big head now from having all these people hanging around you. I do not think you feel a thing. The whole town talks about you like some kind of god. Even I used to think you were some kind of god, maybe even the messiah."

"Right now I do not want a god. I want someone who cares. I need someone who feels. My heart needs someone who has blood in their veins, not ice water."

"You may be a god, but you are not a man. You never have any pain. No one here knows what it will make you cry. You could have saved my brother, who practically worshiped you. Oh, no! You were too obsessed with saving millions."

Jesus reached out to hold them, but they drew back. Cold, bitter pain flew at Jesus from their eyes. They would not let Jesus hold them or touch them.

Jesus' eyes filled with tears at their words. He could feel the anger in their voices and in their eyes. He looked at the floor for a moment, then asked quietly, "Where is he buried?"

Martha snapped "Why go there now? He's been dead three days. He'll be smelling to high heaven now. The time to see him was three days ago, when you might have done something. You could have been here. At least you could have held his hand while he died."

Jesus went to the sandstone cave. Earlier, some friends helped the family bury Lazarus. They rolled a flat piece of stone over the mouth of the tomb. Many generations of the family lay buried there. Eventually, only Lazarus' bones would remain piled with others.

The family sealed edges of the opening with a sand and limestone mud. This kept out burrowing animals and moisture. Jesus broke through the sealer and rolled away the flat stone.

Jesus knelt on both knees in front of the cave, deep in prayer. As he knelt silently, big tears rolled down his cheeks and falling to the ground. It seemed to some who stood by as if Jesus struggled for words.

Martha whispered bitterly to her sobbing sister. "Right now he's probably thinking about what he will look like when he dies. He's wondering how many thousands will come to his own funeral."

The crowd began to grow. Within a few minutes, eight or ten gathered around, watching and waiting. Some stood silently with curiosity and doubt written on their faces. Some eyes showed bitterness toward Jesus' lack of concern. Did he even care about the illness and death of an old friend and supporter?

A few of the crowd jeered. Some made off-color remarks about loyalty. Some openly whispered comments about hypocrisy. Others questioned what Jesus would do with the body. A few questioned Jesus' sanity. Why would a man with a healthy mind open a sealed tomb?

Jesus only said, quietly, "Lazarus, my friend, come out to me."

Lazarus began to stir. As the cloths around him waved, then parted, the crowd suddenly stopped its murmuring. They moved back quickly, letting Jesus kneel alone in silence in front of the tomb.

Lazarus pulled himself out of his own grave. With an unsteady effort, he stood in the door of the grotto. Jesus put his arm around Lazarus to help him stand. The white cloths Mary and Martha had wrapped around his body flapped in the breeze. They were the only remaining evidence of his death.

Lazarus and Jesus and Mary and Martha walked away.

# 49. The Long March
John 2:13-22; Exodus 20:1-17
Following Jesus, but not closely.
Gospel Time: 430

Keli always looked forward to paying his taxes to Levi. Oh, he did not want to part with his money. No, not at all. Keli did not want any of his money to go to Herod's works, either in Jerusalem or even in Galilee.

Though Herod the Great died about 25 years ago, the northern province was still strapped to pay for his projects. Both in Galilee and in Jerusalem, they started the projects before Herod died. Now his heirs and the people they governed must finish the projects.

So Keli paid his taxes, reluctantly of course. K5eli built a home for himself outside Capernaum, about a half mile from the Sea of Galilee. It was a small home, to be sure. Keli lived alone now. His son lived only a hundred yards away with his wife and their teenage son. When Keli made one of his frequent trips to Jerusalem to visit the temple, he felt all right. His grandson stayed in Keli's house to keep it clean and safe.

Every year, Keli went to Levi's tent to pay taxes. Taxes for the maintenance of the roads and armies of the province. Taxes for the roads and armies of Jerusalem.

Taxes to help rebuild the temple of the Jews in Jerusalem. A tax on Keli's house. A tax on this. A tax on that.

Paying that temple tax meant that Keli had every right to visit the rebuilt temple when he was in Jerusalem. He could even help in the rebuilding process, if he chose. Keli knew the temple was in desperate need of rebuilding and purifying. Anything touched by the hand of Herod the Great needed rebuilding and purifying.

Sometimes Keli felt lost in a sea of anonymity. He lived in or around Capernaum and Bethsaida all his life. Yet Keli was among the least well known of all the few thousand who lived in the area. Because he lived outside the walls of the small city, he never sat with the town elders. Keli's wife died ten or fifteen years earlier. Keli was not certain. He could provide his own food from his small garden and from the Sea of Galilee. He had no reason to go to town, except to pay his taxes.

When Keli needed to pay taxes, he bartered for some cloth or leather. Then, using some driftwood, he made a few pairs of sandals. He took these sandals to the town marketplace, the agora. Usually he could sell them all to tourists within a week or so.

Keli came to Levi's tent with his precious coins for the taxes. For several years, Levi and Keli exchanged the same value of coins between them. Some money for the kingdom, and some for the temple. After counting the money, Levi quickly wrote out a note on a small scrap of leather. It simply noted that Keli had paid his assessment.

While Levi wrote, Jesus invited Keli to join the little circle under the tent flap. Jesus, Philo, and three or four others. Men just drifted in and out of the circle as the day went along. This was the part of paying taxes that was enjoyable to Keli, and it was well worth the trouble. He could see his old friends, Levi and Philo, and a few others.

Philo was a special friend to Keli. Philo studied the Greek philosophy and culture often. Whenever a traveler rom Greece or the Decapolis stopped in Capernaum, Philo paid them a visit. He liked the Greek so much he let his friends move back and forth between calling him "Philo" and "Philip." He studied Plato and his concept of the "Ideals." Sometimes he wondered how this might relate to the Jewish thoughts of the Christ. Philo and Keli talked often about the ancient Greek culture still practiced in Scythopolis.

Keli did not know Jesus well, but they had met in the marketplace. Keli knew Jesus shared Keli's heart for the purification of the temple. Keli was not one of the inner group. He just enjoyed being around them. He wanted to spend a little more time with Jesus, but it never worked out. Keli was getting older, now. The walk from his house to the marketplace became longer and more difficult with each visit.

The ancient group known as the Sons of Korah no longer met openly. Keli and Jesus, along with Levi and Philo and many others, shared the vision of the ancients. Keli did sometimes manage to visit the Tent Flap Group. When he did, the purification of the temple was always part of the conversation.

Herod would be the man taking credit for rebuilding the ancient temple. Yet Herod himself was the target of these men of the north who constantly pressed for purification.

Herod the Great claimed to be a Jew, but Judaism rejected Herod the Great. He was born to a family of the deserts of Edom, east of the Jordan River. They took the throne of David's kingdom by force. Now Herod was working to take the high priesthood of the temple by rebuilding the fabulous structure.

Workmen from all the scattered remnants of Judaism came back to Jerusalem to help. Forty-six years of labor went into the temple. Blocks of stone the size of chariots. Massive wooden doors. Marble floors. A roof of oak timbers. Pillars reminded travelers of the great temples of Greece.

To get into the temple itself, one must pass through immense gates. These doors were large enough to admit a huge royal chariot pulled by four horses. Inside the gates stretched the courtyard of the gentiles, large as a football field. In the courtyard of the gentiles, the Jews who were heading for the great sacrificial alter could purchase their supplies. Sheep, doves, every kind of sacrifice called for under temple laws were available.

More than sacrificial elements could be found. Wine, fruit, wheat, nuts, jewelry. They could exchange money from foreign lands for local coins, gold or silver. They would accept only local coins and precious metals at the gift boxes inside, in the courtyard of the Jews. Pilgrims from foreign lands, without coins minted by the Herodians, must exchange their own money for Jerusalem money. The money changers in the courtyard of the gentiles would gladly do this. For a small fee, of course. The courtyard of the gentiles was closer to a tourist trap than a spiritual haven for a faithful people.

In all this glory and money, still the Jews cried for purification. The little group that gathered under Levi's tent flap, almost every day, said little. They knew the purification theme was part of every gathering under the patch of canvas.

As Keli sat next to Jesus in the circle, Jesus told the others the temple purification was on his mind. Jesus said he needed to go to Jerusalem again, just to see what was happening to his beloved temple.

Keli spoke fateful words. "Jesus, if you want to go, just go. I have heard so many people talk about the wonderful things you have done. Many have even said you are the Christ. If you believe you are the Christ, have a little trust. Nothing can happen to you. Even if you are not the Christ, the Lord will protect you if you purify the temple. So just go."

"Listen, my friend. I will tell you this. If you go to Jerusalem, I will go with you. My legs are not good, but I need to make one last trip to Jerusalem. I must go to the temple before I can walk no more. It is time for my trip to Jerusalem for the Passover. Give me two days to be ready, and I will go with you. Perhaps some of these others will be ready as well."

Jesus paused only briefly. "Keli, you are a good man. A little square, perhaps, but a good man. When I go to Jerusalem, many will take offense at my going. Some will wish to destroy me. Even Herod and the High Priest will rise up squarely against me when I move to purify the temple. You are a good man, Keli. In two days, we will go. Who will go with me?" So the word spread quickly. Jesus was getting ready to go to Jerusalem to purify the temple.

Two days later, Jesus appeared again at the tent flap, early in the morning. Several of Jesus' friends, the ones called the Disciples, even slept close by the night before. When Jesus came before the first rays of light crept into the moonless night, the men were already stirring.

When Jesus appeared, one man whispered quietly to another. It might have been an attempt at humor, but no one in this crowd took it as a joke. His voice was quiet, but the power of his invitation covered the crowd. The sound rose above the gentle clamor of men and women preparing for a long trek. "Let's go purify the temple." These words spread down both coasts of the Sea of Galilee ahead of Jesus and the others.

From Capernaum, Jesus led the group down the east side of the sea. Passing through Bethsaida, Jesus paused again briefly at the pool to cleanse himself in its healing waters. Then he moved on.

The group walked only a few hours each day. After the trek they rested at one of the many small towns along the lakefront. At each town, they announced Jesus' trek quietly. Then his mission spread among the people. "Jesus is headed for Jerusalem. There he will purify the temple. Perhaps he will even drive Herod out."

In almost every town, someone answered the unspoken question. "How can the temple ever be pure if Herod's family is controlling it?"

The answer always came back. "It can not be pure if Herod's touch remains."

Three or four days after leaving Capernaum, the last of the disciples caught up with Jesus. He stopped for the others at the point the Sea of Galilee empties into the

Jordan River. An arched bridge spanned the river. Jesus rested after he crossed the bridge.

Some disciples came from towns along the western shore of the Sea of Galilee. When Jesus left Capernaum, one or two of the disciples went south along the western shore. As they passed village after village, they simply passed the word to friends that Jesus was headed to Jerusalem. The word quickly spread to any disciples, his family and any friends that Jesus was on the move to Jerusalem. Everyone knew his mission was to go south to purify the temple.

Jesus intently walked the ancient road through Samaria. At every village and city, well-meaning people seemed to need to judge him and his mission. The Zealots, especially, found cause in their own heritage to question his mission. They wanted to be certain that Jesus followed the ancient ritual laws. If he was to purify the temple, it must be done according to Mosaic law.

In that law, the ritual flow of work must be just so. Lay persons must bring the proper sacrifices. Priests must handle each sacrifice just so. They must handle proper readings from the ancient scriptures just so. Above all, everything must be done decently, and in order. Ceremonial purity was all-important. Yet, the power of the presentation and ritual was critical.

Jesus seemed to take their protests with good humor. In

his mind, the real purity of the temple concerned the relationship between each individual and the Creator. Even the high priest was no better than the warmth of his priestly heart. His ethical standing seemed to falter as he addressed the Lord at the altar.

In Jesus' mind, true faith is a three-way relationship. It is the warm love between the Lord and one's own self; between one's own self and another human; and between that other and the Lord, Jesus himself. It is a triangle of faith, lived out in doing for both Jesus and another human. We define love as those things we do that make our lives the best they can be. The question of purity must then be, "Are these relationships pure?"

After Jesus passed through Jericho, he seemed to enter another zone of his personal mission. From the time he gave Blind Bart back his sight at the west gate of Jericho, Jesus spoke few words.

Keli managed to catch up with Jesus and the others as they walked now up the road. Walking was tough. It was very painful for his knees and hips, but Keli was headed for Jerusalem with Jesus.

He wanted to talk to his friend, Jesus. He wanted to know what was happening inside the mind of this holy man. He wanted to know how Jesus intended to purify the temple. Keli could not ask Jesus anything. Jesus seemed intent on other things, and Keli's mind tried to focus on walking even with the pain.

Keli could not even ask Jesus' mother, Mary, or the other women with the group. They were talking about other things. He could not ask the disciples. Each had their own issues. He could only worry in his heart about what was coming to Jesus – and to himself. Jesus had told them all of the dangers he faced, and the dangers those around him faced. Now as they entered the temple yard, no serious jeopardy seemed likely.

The road winds upward from Jericho to Jerusalem through a series of wadis and along streams. Finally the road rises to the old city of Jerusalem. Long before Jesus climbed the final grade to enter the royal city, he witnessed its presence. He could see the rebuilt peaks of the temple standing tall above the walls. Now Jesus grew even quieter. His back straightened. He seemed to stand a little taller as he prepared himself for his work. Walking into the city, Jesus paused only a moment. He watched the hustle and bustle of the busy city streets a few moments. Then he turned straight to the gleaming temple nearing the finish of its reconstruction.

When Jesus came to the massive gate, he paused. As he knelt in prayer, no one inside the courtyard of the gentiles paid him any attention. Several dozen faithful Jews from every known country bowed in their own meditation inside. Jesus was not anonymous for long.

Jesus walked straight to the steps leading to the courtyard of the Jews. It was over in a flash. Jesus had a mission in his heart. He was ready to carry it out right now. Jesus threw over tables, tossing coins everywhere. He broke open the cages of doves and sheep. As he worked he shouted at the vendors and money changers.

"Get this stuff out of here! You make my Father's house of faith into a house of bargain sales! Stop it, I say, stop it!"

As he spoke, a disciple openly remembered the words Jesus' recalled from ancient scriptures. He spoke them under the tent flap in Capernaum. "Zeal for your house will consume me!"

Some Jews worshiping inside the temple came to Jesus. His actions puzzled them. They wanted to know the problem. They wanted to know why Jesus was tearing down forty-six years of hard work by Herod and by faithful Jews.

Jesus answered them openly. "Destroy this temple, and in three days I will erect it again." These are the words the disciples all remembered later, after Jesus rose from the dead.

Jesus went on into the court of the Jews. As he knelt in prayer, some disciples were with him. Keli did not join Jesus inside. Instead, he found a quiet corner for his own prayer time.

As the ruckus inside calmed down, things returned to normal. The women stayed outside for the moment. When Jesus finally came out, he led his disciples and the women to Bethany.

Keli kept his quiet meditation in the dark corner of the courtyard of the Jews. Here he could ignore the happenings in the open courtyard and on the steps. By the time Keli came out into the light, Jesus and the others were gone. Keli knew which way they went, but he found another way, and another place to stay.

With the pain now overcoming his legs, Keli knew he had to start back to Capernaum immediately. If he tried to rest up and heal a few days, he might never make it home again. So, within a few hours, his tired legs walked again through the massive gates of the temple and the city.

Outside the city gate, he bargained for a ride. Sandals made good bargains. Many caravans passed this way, gathering goods for sale as they went. Within a day or so, Keli had a ride with a military man going to Jericho with orders. From there, he worked his way north with an Egyptian caravan headed for Damascus.

Until his death two months later he often wondered what happened to Jesus. Because he did not hear of Jesus again, he assumed the high priest had ordered him killed. Jesus said this would happen. They would never remember Keli and Jesus in history. They were only human.

# 50. Two Hurting People
## Mark 5:21-43; 2 Sam 1:1, 17-27;
## Psalm 130; 2 Cor 8:7-15
### The impact of Jesus on various lives.
### Gospel Time: 440

Some days and nights of Jesus' life were terribly exciting, frustrating and rewarding. He obviously felt he held in his hands the power and the truth of every bit of creation. The gospels are somehow the story of his impact on the people and the order of the world around him. They spread out from this tiny nation in a highly traveled nation of earth. His impact began almost immediately to touch lives from Ireland to South Africa and Siberia, perhaps even to the Americas.

The gospels are even more than the story of Jesus' impact on world civilizations. They are also the story of Jesus' own struggle with human life. Just like any the rest of us, Jesus had to deal with crowds of people seeking to touch him. They wanted to download some of his miraculous powers through the touch. Most were sincere and honest in their seeking, but perhaps a few acted out of greed.

Today I will tell you a little about two people who acted out of their own desperation. One was desperate to find a cure for her own life-threatening twelve-year struggle. The other sought help and a cure for the struggles of a new twelve-year-old daughter. Working through puberty can be a monumental struggle.

These events were no strangers to Capernaum and Bethsaida. The northern coast of the Sea of Galilee was the ancient equivalent of Yachats, the place of the sacred healers. Dozens of men and women fancied themselves as faithful sacred healers. However, some knew they acted out of fraud and greed as they preyed upon the weak and gullible.

In either case, as they worked their powers, crowds gathered around to download their powers or to watch the spectacles. Some struggled to tough the healers. Some stood a little distance off, hoping to be involved from a distance. Others just walked by slowly, not wanting to appear as if they were interested. Almost everyone who came to the northern shores of the Sea of Galilee came with purpose. They were there because of the legends of healing powers loose in the region.

Into this mass of human hurt and misery stepped the man who would change humanity for all time. The first to approach him for help came forward gingerly. He came out of his own desperate plea for someone to heal his daughter. Twelve years old, and knowing she faced a lifetime of misery from a flow of blood.

Jesus remembered his own twelve year birthday. Joseph and Mary, his parents sponsored him in his manhood ceremonies. Then they asked Jesus if he would like to see Jerusalem on this special occasion. It was time for Joseph to serve his days of priestly responsibility at the temple altar.

Joseph, Mary and Jesus made the long trip to Jerusalem for the most special event of Jesus' young life. As they traveled by foot through the city, they eagerly looked around Jerusalem and the temple. Jesus could only marvel at his own vision for his own life. He knew he would be a dramatic part of the temple, and the people who worshiped there.

Kili had no such dreams for her own life. Her father was a high official at the synagogue. Kili suffered for months with an ailment that disabled most girls for only a few days at a time. She believed, and her father knew, that Kili had no future importance even if she did live through this time.

Jairus brought his wife and daughter to Capernaum a few years ago. His heart spoke a prayer he could find a healer for her. As he walked beside her and the donkey along the way to Capernaum, every step was a prayer. Every step heard Jairus begging the Lord to show him the way to the healer who would save her. "Lord, Blessed art thou, Lord of the Universe, healing of your people. . ."

And on they went.

When the little family reached Capernaum, Jairus could resume his work in the city. He made and repaired chariots for wealthy citizens and for the military. His handiwork cost so much the lower income people could not afford them. In this area, many wealthy families lived, and many high ranking military men served. Jairus could make a good living.

Even that income was not enough to promise Kili a life and a hope for the future. Jairus thought she surely would not survive her childhood. Now as she grew near adulthood and marrying age, Jairus grew desperate. Jairus tried to move closer to Jesus. If only he could attract Jesus' attention, perhaps he could convince Jesus to come to Kili's side. Jesus could lay his hands on her. He could give her a little kiss, or something. Anything which would be the mark of healing on her.

He could not get close to Jesus. Always someone stood between them. It seemed a couple times Jesus looked straight at Jairus with a little compassion. No other sign of recognition.

Then, just as Jairus thought he saw a way to get closer to the prophet and healer, something else happened. Suddenly, Jesus looked startled as he spun around. A very serious look came over his face as he spoke.

"Someone touched me. I know. Someone took power

from me. Who touched me?" Jesus looked over the small crowd.

Marla tried to hide among the people around her, but something in her movements told Jesus Marla was the one. Twelve years of constant blood flow. Twelve years of wondering whether she would live through the night. Twelve years of never touching a man all came to focus when Marla touched the hem of Jesus' robe.

For twelve long years Marla never touched her husband or any other man. He finally left her. Part of his thinking when he married Marla was that she would be part of a great sex life. After a few years, the laws established by Mosaic law caught up with their attraction for each other. She could not touch him because of her blood flow. Finally, he just left. Divorced her. Left Marla devastated and confused.

Marla made her way from Antioch, of Syria, down to Capernaum by the Sea of Galilee. Every man, woman and child of the territory between the Nile River and the Black Sea knew Capernaum. Healers abounded in Capernaum and Bethsaida, the northeastern corner of the Sea of Galilee. They hung around the pool in Bethsaida, working with those waiting for healing. These hopeful people waited to be the first into the pool when the angel should stir the water.

For a small gift, most of these healers were willing to

say their special words for the disabled. Many would offer prayers, or massage with special herbs and oils from far away beyond the sea. For a gift in advance, some guaranteed to carry the disabled into the pool at the right time. Even many who did not claim to be healers earned a fair income in this effort.

Day after day, and through many long nights, Marla waited beside the pool. Most of the time she just sat and prayed. Sometimes she might help other persons move around. Sometimes she talked with others waiting for healing in the sacred waters of the pool. Lately Marla could only begin to feel the desperation of the lonely and the person fated to spend life alone. Death would not be all that bad. She wondered just how long she could lose blood like this.

Marla began to lose hope. She began to even think of ways to hasten her own death. Her loneliness began to take away her faith that the Lord would make her whole one day. Each day she moved a little farther from the pool. Some days she even walked down to the northern shore of the Sea of Galilee. One day, in a bit of self pity, Marla did not return to her little home near the pool. She simply slept under a bush along the road to Capernaum.

In the morning, Marla sat with a few other travelers for breakfast. They ate their tiny meals around a bit of a warming fire. Some berries, a few fish, and a few bites of bread fed the Lord's loneliest. She expected their talk to be of bitterness and loneliness. She listened for thoughts of suicide and frustration.

Today was different. The chatter around the fire was of a new healer who arrived in Capernaum just a few days earlier. He healed often. His words were both strong and gentle. Healing was something he seemed to do without effort. It was a natural outcome of his inside character and relationship with the Lord. Someone suggested the one could be healed by simply touching him.

Simply touching him? Maybe. Maybe Marla had some hope after all. She could probably find him, and touch him. If only she could get close to him.

In Capernaum, Marla quickly learned where she might find this Jesus. Everyone knew him. Outside the tax collector's tent gathered a crowd of several dozen. The ancient law said that she must say the old words whenever she came to a group of people. She must say "Unclean! Unclean!" In Capernaum and Bethsaida, almost everyone was there for the healings. Some came because a priest said that they were unclean. Others came because they could make some money of those who were unclean. So the Herods did not enforce the old laws.

Marla simply took some time to work her way into the center of the crowd. She recognized many who were there. She knew a few of the disabled or ill. She knew others were false healers. Some tried honestly to heal, and occasionally succeeded.

Jesus was just speaking with Jairus about his daughter. Marla stood behind him, but close. As Jesus talked, Marla reached out her hand to touch him. She missed his arm, but did touch the hem of his robe as he lifted an arm. Immediately Jesus stopped talking and turned toward her. Marla already was backing away, afraid of being challenged by this man.

Jesus spoke. "Someone just touched me. I felt the power go out. Who touched me? It was you, right? Did you touch me?"

Marla cringed. She could already feel the lash of the words to come next. She was so desperate she could only shrink from even simple attacks. "Yes, master. I touched you. I have struggled so long. I did not know what to do."

Jesus smiled. "It is all right, Marla. It is all right. Your faith has healed you. When you touched me, your faith with the Lord made you well. Go in peace."

As she walked away, confused by the events, Jairus began to speak. "Jesus, what about Kili, my daughter. She, too, has a bloody flow that will not stop. She is only twelve years old. What am I to do? You can heal her if you choose."

These were the magic words of Jesus. Slowly he turned again toward Jairus. Again, with a smile, Jesus spoke easily, loud enough for the crowd to hear. "Jairus, my friend, your daughter, Kili, will be fine. She is whole already. Go in peace."

Jesus turned away from Jairus. Already others were crowding around, making room for Jairus and Marla to leave, going their different ways. In peace.

# 51. Sylvanus of Gischala
Matthew 22:34-46; Mark 12:28-31,
Luke 10:25-37; Amos 7:7-17
Psalm 90:1-17; Deuteronomy 34:1-12; 1 Thessalonians
2:1-8
An earnest lawyer asks a simple question.
July 10-16   Gospel Time: 450

So often during Jesus' life he dealt with travelers along the highways of Israel. Men and women seemed to drift in and out of his life. This may have been by accident, perhaps not. One of these was Sylvan, a lawyer of Gischala.

The historic image of lawyers has been of wealth and dishonesty. Whether these are true today is debatable.

It was the same in Jesus' time. Neither was necessarily true. For Sylvan, the charges could not be true. He was not a really wealthy man.

Sylvan was a lawyer, all right. Sylvan sat at the city gate, along with the other elders of the city. On certain days the group discussed legal issues of the day. Sometimes the issues were items brought by the community. Property. Inheritance.

Other times the issues were theoretical in nature. What does it mean to adopt? What is the meaning of faith? How can we know true religious practice?

Sylvan sometimes earned some coins representing others before the council at the city gate. The questions presented might be matters of faith, or religion, or military action, or government. Whatever the question, Sylvan tried desperately to find the truth among the issues. It was a personal thing with him. Sometimes he won. Sometimes he lost. Sometimes the little group at the gate of Gischala could only compromise.

Gischala is northwest of Capernaum, about fifteen miles. It was really just a settlement of a couple hundred souls. Sheepherders, traders, crafters, farmers. Several families were quite poor.

Sylvan farmed a few acres along the rolling hills outside Gischala. Grapes, figs, olives and a little grain were his crops. He just held a few acres. Planting, pruning and harvesting the crops took nearly all his time and energy. However, his fields were not the only focus of his life.

His real interest was the law. Sylvan wanted to massage these legal words and phrases into a clear focus on life. His own life and the lives of those around required his work. They needed the order only the law could bring. By his training, Sylvan convinced himself of the need to help community and law work together. Together they should benefit those who called on the

Lord for help.

The law of the day was complex. It rested on a sort of triangle of statutes. The first side of the law was government. The second side was the temple organization as it reached out from Jerusalem. The third side was the military. The military was outside the government. It usually raised its own funds by conscription and attachment. The military even chose its own battles.

Each of these had its own set of laws, established by its own powerful people. Life of people like Sylvan was simple, with an easy guideline. Avoid the laws established by the government, the temple and the military. No democracy was left from the ideals of the Greeks. Democracy would not live again until the time of Jefferson and Franklin and Washington.

The assumption was that every person accepted the few points that hold civilization together. First, every individual and community must have a relationship with the Lord. Second, the community also needed a corporate war process. A third point must set up community action such as roads, walls and wells.

Not in the pyramid, though, were two other main pieces of the world. We expect to find them at the center of law. Business to business matters, and individual rights were just left to hang loose in society. Fend for yourself was the essential law in both instances.

Business and individual had some protection in the law, however. It was just that neither business nor individual had any real possibility of claiming victory. If any made claim against the government, the military, or the temple, the citizen lost.

Between business and business, or individual and individual, strong laws kept good order. The lawyers of the day focused on these matters at the city gate. Almost every city of the world ran itself this way.

Property matters and damages were a prime focus. Criminal actions and minor disagreements took part of the time. Deeply personal issues such as health and emotional problems headed the issues. They required consideration by the elders of the city. Leprosy and blindness were among the most difficult issues for the group.

All these matters required straight thinking by the most respected minds of the community. Any issue could come from any person to the council of elders. The gospels frequently refer to decisions made by these councils. Often the leaders chose areas of discussion that gave Jesus areas for irony or disagreement.

For the people involved in these councils, training for a legal career was personally motivated. A man had four primary methods of learning. Observation, reading, reciting or discussing the law, and trial and error were important. These divisions of study made law very exciting for Sylvan. Sylvan carefully followed all these throughout his career.

Sylvan watched carefully the community around himself. He could see the impact of the law on people. He learned to read at the synagogue. He practiced reading from the Torah and the scrolls of the prophets and the psalms. Sylvan made presentations of legal issues to his friends and family. Eventually he spoke before the elders.

Then he began to work through the trial and error procedures brought to the council. He questioned and contemplated. The detail-oriented Sylvan composed solutions, and rewrote them. The lawyer in him watched the others carefully. Sylvan tried to note their response to various statements and issues. Finding the truth was most important.

It is here that Sylvan's life becomes really interesting to us in the current century. Sylvan's life did not become so famous as that of Jesus, or Nero, or Paul. Sylvan is almost anonymous.

We reach back another thousand years, past Jesus, to find Sylvan's impact on our world.

Very few people know anything about Amos. Amos lived most of his life in the hills north of the Sea of Galilee. He wandered north of Gischala and Capernaum. His work was as a shepherd and farm laborer. He says he was not a prophet, but the world remembers him as one.

Three or four hundred years before Amos, in about 1100 B.C., we find our clue. Moses and Aaron brought the Hebrew people through the wilderness toward Jericho. In the wilderness things went badly for the Hebrews. Starvation sat in, and the people were becoming very discouraged.

Moses and Aaron knew things were going badly for the Hebrews. They said it was because some people were doubting the team of Moses and Aaron. It was the sort of stand we have seen in other world leaders. We have even seen it in our own churches and denominations.

The man Korah and some others then challenged Moses and Aaron on their words. Korah could not accept that the Lord had made this appointment. Moses and Aaron claimed to be commanders and priests of the entire nation. Korah and his people appeared at the tents of Moses and Aaron one day. A large group of supporters came with them.

Korah and other men challenged Moses and Aaron on their claims of ordination. They claimed the Lord appointed them commanders and priests of the entire nation. What happened next?

We are not really certain. Moses and Aaron apparently had Korah and his people killed and buried in the desert.

Over the next centuries, faithful thinkers developed a way to challenge such power. Mostly from the north, they established a group movement of citizen prophets. These people found constant ways to challenge whatever government was in power at the time. They usually called for a return to a life of justice and righteousness. Amos became one of these in about 750 B.C. From that day to this, the Sons of Korah have challenged us. They changed the way we look at folks' self-pronouncement of a call to authority.

Sylvan also became a son of Korah. This strong religious order served at the time of Jesus. Strong men and women filled northern Palestine. They were willing to risk their lives for justice and righteousness. How did this change our lives?

Sylvan often made business and religious trips to Capernaum. The custom rose to invite visitors to be honorary elders for the day. Any who sat among the elders elsewhere could sit with the elders here. Sylvan became a well known and accepted member of the elders at the Capernaum gate.

The problems Sylvan and the other elders tried to resolve were many-sided and deep. Spiritual matters were most troubling. These were not matters of temple power or strategies. They were matters of the relationship between individuals and the holy one. Then as now, the most pressing of these questions was the matter of eternal life.

Many elders could and did ask and answer questions. They made comments as individuals and as small groups. They could share in any refreshments passed around. Figs. Grapes. Raisins. Bread. Tea. Wine.

Sitting with the elders at Capernaum this day, Sylvan responded to legal needs for answers. Jesus came to the city and stopped at the gate. Sylvan thought this might be an opportunity to get fresh insight.

Sylvan did not know much about Jesus. He had only heard rumors about the man. These rumors intrigued him enough that Sylvan took them seriously. Sylvan happened to be at the Sea of Galilee a few days. He found the opportunity to question Jesus irresistible. Sylvan could not consider the rumors for himself in the light of the law.

The rumors Sylvan wanted to clarify with Jesus really threatened Galilean society. All culture of Israel was up for grabs, according to the rumors.

One rumor had it that Jesus intended to change the ten commandments. Sylvan also heard that Jesus had edited the shema. Jesus' editing might be simply quoting old statements of the law. "You will love the Lord, your god. You will love with all your heart, and mind, and soul and strength. You will love your neighbor as yourself."

This was confusing to Sylvan. How could this be wrong? It only repeated old thoughts.

Jesus did work on the sabbath. Is healing, or doing the

ordinary functions of life, really work? Regardless, the law should approve. How could it be wrong to eat an ordinary meal?

Politically, the rumors said Jesus led a revolt against the king or against Rome itself. Sylvan looked around at the few men who seemed to walk and talk with Jesus. He could see no evidence of military action, or weapons, or even covert action. Nothing showed any sign of Jesus' casting fear into the heart of the Roman government. The mightiest government and military of the world should have no fear of this man.

The rumors said Jesus turned families against each other. Well, maybe. Sylvan could see how families could disagree with one another about what Jesus said. Then Jesus did, apparently, ask people to go with him, to walk with him. They might have to leave their families to go with Jesus. Sylvan supposed this could be a problem.

The most serious rumor and challenge to Jesus rose from this gathering. The trouble lay in the charge that Jesus suggested they ignore the temple mandates. Thinking outside the box about salvation raised questions. The temple must define and describe salvation for the people. If it could not, how could the nation live? Even the government, the military and business of the day faced terrible challenges.

Sylvan could think of only one question to ask. That

query really brought all these issues and rumors together. If Jesus answered it, Sylvan knew just what it was Jesus was about. Sylvan knew Jesus was not trying to challenge the law. He did not seem to push on the government or the temple. The hierarchy saw no reason to fear the revolt Jesus might have planned.

So Sylvan worked his way close to Jesus in the crowd. At a quiet moment, Jesus looked straight at Sylvan. He apparently expected a question or a statement from the learned man. Something about that eye contact invited Sylvan to find some way to walk with Jesus. Jesus seemed to push for a closer contact with the lawyer.

Sylvan did not hesitate. He asked Jesus the obvious basic spiritual question of that day or any other. "Teacher, what must I do to have eternal life?"

Jesus answered with a question Sylvan did not expect. "You have read the law. What does it say in the law?"

The legal man answered quickly. "You shall love the Lord, your god, with all your heart, mind, soul and strength. You shall love your neighbor as yourself."

Jesus spoke quietly now. "You are correct. Go and do this. Life is waiting for you."

Sylvan was ready for this response. "Sir, who is my neighbor?"

Again, Jesus apparently had prepared well. He smiled at the question. "A man was going down from Jerusalem to Jericho. Along the road, robbers attacked him. They stripped him and beat him, and ran away. They left the man for dead. Now, luckily a priest was going down that road. When he saw the man, he walked on the other side of the road. Soon a Levite, seeing the man, walked by on the other side of the road."

"A Samaritan, walking home from Jerusalem through Jericho, came to the man. When the Samaritan saw the man, he had compassion on the victim. The Samaritan bandaged the wounds. He poured expensive oil and wine on the wounds. Then he sat the victim on the Samaritan's own donkey. The traveling Samaritan brought the victim to the inn in Jericho. The Jericho inn was the best facility to take care of him. The next day he gave two large coins to the innkeeper. 'Take care of him. If it costs more, I will be back in a few days to pay.'"

Now Jesus looked Sylvan in the eye again. "Which of these three, do you suppose, was neighbor to the man who was beaten?"

Sylvan now was in awe. Jesus, in his parable, invited Sylvan to share the depth of his commitment to Israel. Sylvan answered, and accepted the invitation. "The one who showed mercy on the fallen man."

Jesus said to him, simply, "You go, then, and live the same life."

Though Sylvan returned to Gischala, he walked with

Jesus all the days of his life.

Sylvan accepted the burden of sharing creative genius with the Lord. He knew the redemption of the Christ and the presence of the Spirit. His act of faith has changed our lives. His question gave Jesus the opportunity to invite many to faith. Jesus also gave much more specific instructions to us.

"Go! Live the life of the good Samaritan."

## 52. The Gift
Mark 10:46-52; Matthew 9:27-31; Luke 18:35
Psalm 34:1-22; Job 42:1-17; Hebrews 7:23-28
Eyes that see are Jesus' gift to Bart.
October 23-29      Gospel Time: 460

Most of us want notice. Some try hard to make something happen around themselves. However, few people ever created less stir with their life than did Bartimaeus. Most people around him knew him only as `Blind Bart'.

Blind Bart was a fixture on the road that goes up from Jericho to Jerusalem. Rich and poor, natives and travelers, families and armies alike knew him by sight. One trip up the little canyon toward Jerusalem introduced travelers to the pest. They traveled the road Blind Bart guarded with his cries for assistance. Sometimes they even avoided making the trip. Bart was such a nuisance on the road! Sometimes they went around by a much longer and riskier route. They just wanted to avoid meeting him.

Blind Bart never had much of a life. All day Bart sat on the edge of the road calling out for help. He called for someone to come. He begged everyone for food or clothing or shelter. He called out to every passerby. With the whiniest voice, he begged. He only wanted them to lay some coins in the wooden bowl. That bowl was his kitchen. The bowl was also his wash basin, his collection plate and his friend.

For nearly all of his forty years Blind Bart begged. He just lived off the good will or the sympathy of others. His life as a begger made him a parasite, not supporting himself at all. On this day he heard people talking and arguing from the heart. What they said may not have given him hope. However, it did make him curious.

The people who passed by talked about a man coming up the winding road. They called the man the "messiah" and "son of David." Some thought maybe even "king of the Jews" was appropriate.

King of the Jews! If this stranger really was the king of the Jews, this was an opportunity. The man controlled the lives and fortunes of all the people. He could hand out large sums of taxpayers' money on a whim. Surely a blind man could get some of that loot with the right effort.

Bart was ready. He made sure his clothes were just properly dirty and torn, but not too smelly. He checked his bowl for just a hint of crusty dirt.

When Jesus came near, Blind Bart started calling out. He used just the right voice of sadness and pain. "Jesus, son of David, have mercy on me! Jesus, help me!"

The people around Bart knew what he was up to. He was calling Jesus to answer Bart's begging. They said

"Shush!" They said "Be still. How can Jesus deal with you? Who cares about you anyway? We know your tricks!"

Someone said "If Jesus claims to be the king of the Jews, fine. If he gives some coin to this parasite, I do not want to be around. I do not want to be around a man taken in by such a fraud."

"Jesus! Son of David! You will go to Jerusalem to claim your throne. Help me right here, today!"

Jesus said "Someone call him to come here. I will talk with him."

They called out, "Bart, come here. Jesus will talk with you now. Hurry! None of your tricks!"

Bart sprang to his feet, forgetting even his wooden bowl. He pressed his way through the crowd to where Jesus stood. His eyes now focused on Jesus. Jesus met those eyes now seeing but not realizing they were seeing. He said "What should I do for you?"

Something about the way Jesus watched caused Bart to change his plea. His cry for alms and support became a cry for eyes that worked.

He had tried this before, asking for eyes that could see. When the passers-by could not oblige, they were embarrassed. They could not supply him with seeing eyes. They were so embarrassed and felt so guilty somehow. These men of the world came through with money instead. Bart felt guilty as well.

As Bart made his plea, he realized he could see. His eyes slowly focused on Jesus. Jesus said "Look, man, look! Because you asked, I have given you your eyes! Is there something else you want?"

Bartimaeus was afraid, but not afraid of Jesus. He lost all thought of this strange man. Now Bart was afraid for his life. Now he was afraid for himself in a new way. No more could he practice his career. Gone was the only life he knew, the life of a beggar. No more crying for alms. Enough pity from passers-by. No more attempts by those who knew him to pass by quietly.

Now Bartimaeus had responsibility. Hard work now came from completely new directions. Bart knew a completely new life. Bartimaeus doubted he could handle it. Jesus knew. Jesus knew Bart's character.

Bart closed his eyes, and opened them just to see if they were really working. He looked at the crowd and at his own hands and clothing. Again he closed his eyes in wonder. He savored the moment, the expectation, the excitement. Even the questions of his own future excited him. He thought about Jesus. Quickly Bart opened his eyes to see the man who had given him new life.

Jesus turned away now. Someone else needed his attention. He moved on up the road to Jerusalem and to his own destiny. Just for a moment their eyes met, and Jesus smiled. Then he was gone.

## 54. Entering Paradise
## Luke 18:15-17
More people in the circle of faith.
Gospel Time: 465

Isaiah, son of Lampo and Marcia, had so many questions. Every morning, on rising, Isaiah left his bed with a commitment to live out the power of his namesake. A morning time of prayer and meditation lifted his senses out of their nighttime fog. He prayed for his family, for the temple, and for the messiah to come. He prayed for his home town, the village of Nob, and for the synagogue. These prayers and the expected response from the Lord were both his responsibility and his birth right.

Six centuries earlier, the first Isaiah lifted his prophetic voice in both condemnation and promise of the people called Israel. That Isaiah spoke of the Lord's bitterness toward city-states all over the area. He said that Israel and all her neighbors together would be wiped out for their violation of the will of the Lord. Their ethics, their greed, their violence and their injustice were just cause for destruction in the name of the Lord.

But that first Isaiah knew the Lord would not just destroy. He would also redeem, lift up, heal, bring to life again. When Israel was given freedom to return to the

Promised Land, people remembered Isaiah. They remembered his prophecies about freedom and release.

Now the new Isaiah, the little Isaiah, at ten years age, began to feel the power of those same words. Every day he thought on the condemnations and prophesied release spoken by the Isaiah of old times.

Every day, now, he went to the door of the synagogue. Even as a young boy he was allowed to sit near the circle of elders as they discussed the weighty theological and social issues of the day. Every day someone quoted some passage from the Torah. Always someone added something from at least one prophet. Always someone added a psalm, a prayer, or something from the writings of Job, Proverbs or Ecclesiastes.

Then for some time, the group traded questions and statements about the matters brought up in those passages. What did this mean? How could it have been said differently? It meant something centuries ago. Does it still mean the same thing? Does it reveal different values and principles?

Young Isaiah began to feel his own power in the statements and questions. He began to see how the simple faith of a child can be a powerful force in the synagogue and community. Although he was not allowed to ask questions of the entire group yet, there were other ways he could use that power.

Whenever some issue or discussion raised something within him, he voiced his question to his father or to one of his uncles in the group of elders. Often that man answered the boy directly. Then the man repeated the question and his answer to the group as a whole. Sometimes that response was enough.

At other times, the group of elders debated the young Isaiah's issues with every bit of urgency they used with the elder Isaiah's prophetic words. While they rarely spoke directly to young Isaiah, they carefully assured themselves he understood the matter. It was their gift to him, and to the Lord, and to the future of Israel.

One day, Isaiah's friends were playing with a leather-covered ball of wool. Sometimes they played simple games of catch. Other times, they played keep-away. Or they hit the ball with sticks. They thought up many games for entertainment and exercise.

Usually, Isaiah stayed to listen to the elders a long time. But when the council finished for the day, Isaiah was ready to move on. He usually heard other boys and girls playing some place close. Which game they were playing did not matter. Isaiah knew only it was time for some excitement to wake him up.

Sometimes, one or two of the men in the council made crude remarks about the noise the youngsters made as they played close to the council. If the counsel stayed in session too long, the children began their games. They were noisy, and this upset some of the council. Often one of the men spoke of Isaiah, wishing the other children were more like Isaiah. They thought he was more respectful of his elders. He usually waited until they were finished before he ran off to play.

Today, however, Isaiah was trapped into leaving a bit early. Just as the elders began to close their session, the leather ball bounced into the group. Lampo, Isaiah's father, caught the ball with one hand.

Lampo studied the ball momentarily before speaking. "Look at this. The ball is in my hand. No, it is in all our hands. We are responsible for the work of the Lord now. All of Creation is for us to use and to maintain and improve. But someday we will die. All of us. Someday we will all be gone. Then, all of this will be the responsibility of another generation."

Lampo gestured as if to toss the ball to others in the council. Then he drew back. Finally, he tossed the ball easily to Isaiah.

By this time, other boys and girls came running up looking for their ball. Now gathered around the outside of the circle, they stood and waited for Lampo to finish his words. Then they waited for Isaiah to come play with them.

Before Lampo's toss reached Isaiah, Isaiah knew the

point his father was trying to make with Isaiah, with the other youths, and with the other members of the council. Isaiah saw his own future and the future of the entire community would soon be in the hands of his generation. He knew he must be ready.

Isaiah also knew his questions and answers with the council, as well as his play with the other boys and girls, were important. They trained him in his role as a leader in the community. They also were his powerful tools. He needed them as he worked. He could use them to carefully shape Israel and the world toward his understanding of the Lord's vision.

Isaiah quickly stood and threw the ball to a friend standing some distance away from the group. The boys and girls ran toward him, laughing and shouting as they went. Isaiah went with them.

One of those who often grumbled about the noise made by the youngsters spoke now. "See what I mean? Even young Isaiah can not sit still if he has a chance to go play. What do you think of that, Lampo? Is your boy going to grow up some day?"

Lampo paused a moment before beginning his answer. Just as he opened his mouth to speak. Lampo saw something else which gave him opportunity to stall for time.

For several months, now, the little village of Nob had

known of a new healer from the north. His name was Jesus, son of the carpenter from Nazareth, Joseph.

This Jesus had moved from Nazareth to Capernaum a few years ago. He found work as a carpenter. The work of a carpenter seemed to be a good task for his skilled hands.

However, after a few years, Jesus began to heal persons around Galilee. Chorazin, Capernaum and Bethsaida served as the base of operations for his new career. As time went on, Jesus worked less and less as a carpenter and more and more as a healer.

The three cities at the north end of the Sea of Galilee were famed for their healing resorts and their professional healers. Ill persons from all over the region came in by caravan, traveling alone, or by family, to find those miraculous cures. They came from all over the Roman empire. From Morocco, or Britain, or India or Scandinavia; they came to find healing.

As they came, each found some healer. As they returned to their homeland, they talked about that one who made them whole. If they were not satisfied, they spoke of that as well. In very short order, the word about the healer Jesus spread around the Roman world.

By this time, Jesus' fame as a healer became mixed with his push for temple purity and righteousness. The rebels of the Galilean hills, the Sons and Daughters of

Korah, adopted Jesus' call to purity in Jerusalem. Building on fame from his healing powers, the Korahites talked Jesus up as one who could and would restore the purity of the temple in Jerusalem.

This was a good time to purify the temple. The family of Herod the Great were leading the rebuilding of the majestic building. With stones the size of chariots, and statues the size of horses, it would be a draw to faithful Jews everywhere. It might even be a challenge to the healing resorts of the north.

Some people of Nob said that Herod's great tax, about thirty years earlier, was levied as a means of gathering money from the Jews of areas around the world. The money would be used for rebuilding the temple. The tax was also a means to bring people and money to Jerusalem, away from tourist traps such as Chorazin, Capernaum and Bethsaida. The resentment toward this tax now lived on for thirty years, driving rebellion toward the Romans and the Herodians for centuries among the hill people of Galilee.

Thirty years later, this bitter hurt fit right into Jesus' ambition to see Jerusalem one day. After gathering a small group of followers, Jesus started for Jerusalem. Down along the Sea of Galilee, also known as Lake Tiberias, along the Jordan River, through Jericho, up toward Jerusalem through Nob. Jesus moved slowly but intently. He stopped and talked at many towns along the way to explain his thinking and his work.

Finally reaching Nob, Jesus seemed content to enter for rest, food and conversation. As he entered the little community, Jesus walked toward the synagogue. The town knew of his coming. The spreading missionaries had done their work well. As he walked with his people, others just seemed to step into the parade. Even the boys and girls playing with the leather-covered ball stopped their game and followed along.

As Jesus neared the synagogue, the kids began to ask the questions they heard earlier from their parents. "Are you Jesus, the miracle worker from Galilee?" "Will you clean up the temple?" "Will you drive Herod out?" "Will you heal Jabosh? He has a crooked arm. A chariot ran over him when he was little." "If we walk with you, will take us to heaven?"

Jesus seemed to enjoy answering their questions. He smiled a lot, and gave many hugs. Isaiah moved closer to Jesus. "Jesus, my name is Isaiah. Do you know who the old Isaiah was?"

Now Jesus smiled even more, but with a serious look in his eyes. "Yes, Isaiah, I know the old Isaiah. His words have given me much understanding and power. They have helped me understand who I am."

"So, Jesus, if Isaiah has helped you understand who

you are, just who are you? Some people say you are the world's greatest healer. Some say you will drive Herod out, along with the Romans when you purify the temple. But I think you are the messiah. Are you?"

Jesus only responded simply to Isaiah. "You have said that with your own words. It could be so, if you say it is."

Now the men of the council began to feel uncomfortable with this line of questioning. They knew these were fighting words. Herod's spies would be delighted to report this to Herod. They had to get rid of the nuisance.

"Hey, kids, leave Jesus alone. You are too young to know about such things. Go back to your ball game. We will talk to Jesus, then tell you about him. That is all you need to know."

"Awww, for crying out loud. Let us talk to him. If we are to be the leaders after you die, we need to learn about people like Jesus."

Now Jesus entered the conversation again. He seemed to get his old strength back. His voice showed his frustration with the old guard of the Nob synagogue council.

"Let them be. These young men and women are friends of mine. They are asking the good questions because they want to know about me. They are not asking just to build up their power. They just want to know."

"I will tell you the truth. These kids are trying hard to enter the kingdom through the doors of faith; you are trying to block them. You men are trying hard to drive them away. They will have the kingdom because of their faith. But if you men do not learn to accept them into your world as they have accepted me into theirs, you will never enter the kingdom of heaven."

"Your words tell all of us about you. You will welcome children as you welcome the kingdom of heaven. I have seen how you welcome children. It makes me sad. Will you welcome the kingdom of heaven the same way? Now, I will be here a few hours before I go on to Jerusalem. What shall we talk about?"

Now Isaiah and his friends sat down inside the council circle. For the next few hours, Jesus talked with his new friends in the circle of faith. Then he moved on toward Jerusalem.

# 55. Frustrated Parade Marshall
Luke 19:28-40; Matthew 21:1-9; Mark 11:1-10;
Psalm 31:9-16; Isaiah 50:4; Philippians 2:5-11
Judas arranges things.
Sunday before Easter        Gospel Time: 470

This fellow we know walked with Jesus since the earliest days of the movement. He was not the first to come on board. Others came before him. However, he was in the first and most devoted group.

Our hero had at first been an outsider. He was something of a loner. After time and after putting a great effort into Jesus' work, Judas was ready. He was finally a trusted part of the inner circle.

Now, on the long trip to Jerusalem, he could showcase his work. His ability to handle details of lodging and housing and support was really paying off. The organizer seemed able to find just the right accommodations. This kept the tiny band of wanderers from coming unglued entirely.

His work was unsung. Few apart from Jesus paid any attention to his successes and his toil. He knew he was working his way into a position of strength within the group. This was important.

As the little band gathered in every town, people came to see Jesus. They wanted healing, or just to be around Jesus, or to challenge his authority. They wanted to invite him to their home for dinner or to spend the night.

First, though, anyone who wanted to see Jesus had to deal with this fellow. He had things organized and wanted to keep them that way. He had an elaborate little system of procedures, simple yet adequate. This kept things on an even businesslike keel.

These procedures helped ensure stability. When they left even the larger towns the small band went on in peace. Thus they left behind the citizens of the smaller towns. Those towns now wondered for months who had really been among them.

When they were out on the road again, the group had work to do. Our hero picked up the pieces and made the group ready for the next town. He told them about the town, who was important who was not. He went to various disciples to tell them of a specific person to visit. Many were special to the mission, in Judas' mind.

Then, while the group was in town, our man double-checked everyone's assignments. He then began to prepare for the next community. He had worked all these communities before. In the short period he had traded in the area, he visited all these communities. He personally knew just about every important person in the nation.

Now he had an opportunity to put those old acquaintanceships to good purpose. He was very good at what he did. Jesus knew he needed this man for the mission.

Jerusalem was a huge challenge. It was much larger than the other towns they visited, larger even than Jericho. This ancient city held more wealth, more power, many more self-claimed important people. Many persons resisted relocation by a forceful intruder from the north.

It was not an impossible task. Judas knew he was up to it. With any kind of luck the little group will survive Jerusalem in good order. They will make their visit to the temple as a pilgrimage. The group will burn their incense and call it a day. The disciples will sacrifice a dove or two on most days. Perhaps he could locate a lamb during the Passover festival. They might even celebrate the Passover together as a family before they left town. Our man knew readiness to leave quickly was critical. He also knew Jesus and the others were committed to be in Jerusalem at Passover.

"Next year in Jerusalem!" This rallying cry of the Hebrews at Passover lived since the days of the captivity. Dozens of generations of families have gone by since that disaster. Many families have not seen any member able at the temple during these holy days. Many of these men and women will never have another opportunity.

This was the great opportunity for some. It can be done properly if everyone just stays in step.

Probably the person most likely to get out of line was Jesus himself. The prophet did things on his own that frustrated the best of Judas' plans. One could not complain too much. After all, Jesus was the central figure of this whole parade.

Our organizer was confident. Had he not brought the group this far safely? His plans were ready. Even the procession to the temple was ready. In his mind he could see the great drama of the messiah's arrival.

First, two or three disciples walked carrying banners proclaiming the salvation of the nation. Then the other disciples came walking in order of age. Our man tried to design a marching order that recognized some rank within the organization. He deserved it, but he knew the others did not go for this. Their egalitarian spirit deeply frustrated him.

Popularity was all right in this instance. The disciples moved around greeting people. They let the world know their faces and voices. They kissed the babies and teased the children. They might even carry a banner proclaiming "This year in Jerusalem!".

Then in Judas' vision, Jesus came riding a chariot. Judas could arrange this with a local friendly chariot rental service. Judas allowed none of the rent-a-junker stuff, either. This had to be first class.

Then women and anyone of lower class who wanted to join came at the end.

Then on to the temple. Judas' vision showed the great welcome spontaneously erupting when the crowd recognized who was coming.

Oh, yes, our hero. He must not be directly in the parade. He was much too busy for participation. Besides, marching was for the ordinary folk, like Simon and James. Our man still had trouble with the nickname Jesus had placed on Simon. No one should respond to the silly word "Peter." Calling him "The Rock" seemed to refer to the state of Simon's mind.

With the procession, our hero marched proudly, moving forward and back. He walked slightly to the side, keeping the whole organization in order. Someone had to check the timing and speed and discipline for maximum crowd effect. The faces of the crowd reveal every possible response.

Of course, they would probably ask him to sign a few autographs. He did not really mind.

You could guess it. Some things went wrong and our hero was nearly frantic.

First, the chariot was not there on time. Jesus insisted he ride a donkey. One disciple found it tied at the gate of the city. Oh, the horror of it! The son of man, the king of the Jews, riding a jackass!  This embarrassment rather than the royal $400 per hour chariot that they had already contracted!

This was not a typical Jerusalem crowd. The Jews had an ancient rallying cry of the people at Passover. "Next year in Jerusalem." Many people in the distant towns took Jerusalem at this time of year very seriously.

Then, because the visitors came as pilgrims, additional crowds of beggars and thieves showed up. Others brought out trinkets and fast food and hats and even palm branches. The pilgrims were easy marks as they neared the temple. Pilgrims have always been tempting targets.

In the milling around, in the confusion, the crowd started gathering without any order. The disciples who were to lead the procession lost their banners to beggars or thieves. Someone was always looking for clothing. These people stole anything!

Many disciples tore palm fronds off the closest trees. They just needed something to wave.

Worse than that, by the time the branches were ready, Jesus started toward the temple. He was just beginning to press his way through the mob of people. These were not the dignitaries of the city who should have been at the parade. The riffraff who gathered just wanted to see what the excitement was. The disciples could only follow along and wave their palm branches in the air.

Other people saw the branches. Some thought this looked like a good thing. It was a traditional parade activity for the Jews, of course. Boys quickly scampered up the trees and cut more branches. They sold the fronds to the parade watchers and marchers. The fronds were good for waving and for fanning.

Soon the whole mob was just sort of slowly stampeding its way toward the temple. It moved at the slow pace of a less-than-eager donkey. At first, no one really knew why they were going to the temple.

All the slogans our hero drilled into the disciples were lost. The disciples scattered among the crowd of tourists and beggars and palm branch sellers. Finally someone picked up an easy one that seemed to stick. Shouts of "Hosanna!" and "Here comes the king" sounded through the crowd. Then the crowd began to suspect the meaning of the parade.

Joining a parade is easy. Joining is risky if you are the one who pays if the parade scatters.

Our poor hero, now struggling to keep up with the crowd, was simply lost. He wasted all this planning and all his struggles. They trampled all his weeks of thought and preparation. These undisciplined new followers of Jesus just made a mess of things. They did not even know his name!

Our man was heartbroken. He began to make rude

comments about the clumsy newcomers. This mob made the parade their parade. He scorned the wandering disciples who did not help him get things organized.

This illiterate mob with no sense of timing was destroying all of Jesus' work. They simply had no idea what was appropriate action around the son of man. He might be the king of the Jews, the one who belonged on the throne. The crowd did not know how to treat him.

Our hero began to curse this mob that forced him out to the sidelines. The excited men and women pushed and shoved as they tried to approach Jesus. The rumor quickly spread that he was the one bringing the kingdom of the Lord.

Judas cried "But this is not right! Get back in line! This is supposed to be a royal parade! It is not a street dance after a victory by some gladiators!"

Grabbing and holding, Judas tried and failed to convince marchers to follow the pattern so carefully laid out. Judas could not get these new followers of Jesus into his well-planned parade. Our hero became very frustrated. He wanted to shake from his feet the dust of the whole mess.

At last one woman lost her patience. She had been trying to get past our man for several minutes. As the parade moved yelled in his ear, she yelled at Judas. The whole crowd could have heard her voice. "If you do not want to move along with Jesus, stand aside. Do not block the parade! Do not block those of us who want to be with him! If you do want to move with Jesus, join the parade. Do not gripe about it! Join the parade or move over!"

What? Join the parade? A demand to join the parade? Our hero who had masterminded the whole thing? Our hero who laid the best plans? Well, circumstances had forced them to be laid aside.

This guide who led the group from the beginning? A ten minute follower of Jesus now told our hero to join the parade!

They were ignoring our hero with deep credentials of long standing. They were pushing the months of trial serving Jesus and his ministry aside.

Now, with the rabble clearly taking over the procession, Judas had to act. This mob must not control the entire process of Jesus' ministry. Judas tried to force the crowd and Jesus to make the shift. These new followers must move on from operating as a rampaging mob. The crowd had to become a steady body for the new kingdom.

He had only one way to shock this crowd to its senses. The mob must come to their knees in the face of some great miraculous event.

He saw Jesus do miracles. Judas witnessed the lame start walking. Our man witnessed the blind regain their sight. He was there at the feeding of the five thousand. He knew what Jesus could do, if only Jesus could be forced into action.

The problem was Jesus, himself. Jesus must be forced to do the greatest miracle of all time. This must bring the whole nations to its knees in front of its new king.

So our hero made his plan. He began laying out in his minds the actions and responses. Judas was certain these would finally lead to the greatest miracle. The state must hold a trial, perhaps even an attempted execution. At the last second, Jesus must save himself. When Jesus walked away, it would be complete. Everyone everywhere would finally know this fellow was the rightful king of the Jews.

The confusion and clamor of the rabble grew. The mob loudly escorted Jesus to the great temple of the Lord. Quietly, Judas Iscariot drifted away from the disciples.

# 56. Widow's Tiny Gift
## Mark 12:38-44; Luke 21:1-7
### Psalm 127; Ruth 3:1-5, 4:13-17; Hebrews 9:24-28
Some folks have much to give.
November 6-12     Gospel Time: 480

Jesus made his trip slowly. It was the last long journey of his life. His small band came down from the hill country to the southern territories of Palestine. The group met Zacheus in Jericho and shared a meal with him. Bartimaeus regained his sight at the hands of Jesus. Then Jesus left Jericho to come up the hill to Jerusalem.

Now in the holiest city of all Jesus stood quietly. He surveyed the most holy building in all the world, the great temple. Jesus' soul pondered its beauty and majesty. Its presence and design reflected the sentiment of the Jewish people. Their Lord was the god of the entire universe. Even the beauty of a temple rebuilt by Herod could be useful to the Lord.

Carved stones and hanging drapes caught everyone's eye. Gold statuary and ornaments graced the gateways and door posts and walls. The builders embedded emeralds and rubies in their work. Throughout the many doors and columns, precious stones met the faithful as they gathered.

Into this majestic scenario came hundreds and sometimes thousands of people on a daily basis. They came to make sacrifices and prayers. Studying the Torah and talking to the priest were almost worth the pilgrimage. They came because this was the holiest of holy places.

On this day the son of the Lord was teaching in the temple. The son of the Lord was teaching in the temple but this was not enough. Marian came to the temple and made her gift because she cared.

Some might say this was not an easy thing for Marian to do. Some said Marian really had to force herself to give this way. Many said that, but it was not true. Forcing herself to give was not in the way of Marian.

It had been twelve long years since her husband, Stalyk, had died. For twelve years, Marian made this trip, day after day after day.

It was not a long trip, only a few minutes, perhaps half a mile. The walk was a pleasant interlude on the hill. Even in the heat of the day, Marian felt good around the temple. On the hottest days she shaded herself with the hood of her robe.

At first she noticed all the people along the route. She spoke to them as she passed. The people of the street came to expect her to walk by each day. Shopkeepers, beggars, children and others, like herself, just kept on keeping on.

Now she simply walked, and kept walking. She always tried to keep her mind on two things. Visiting the temple and serving her friends on made her feel important.

Stalyk was a shoe maker, a sandal maker, a leather and wood worker by trade. He was very good at making sandals. Many wealthy people came to him for sandals. Many poor came, as well. Stalyk sold all he could make.

Sometimes they called on Stalyk to make harness for horses or donkeys. Sometimes, when he had time to spare, he made leather and wood shields for soldiers.

Stalyk was a good man, a strong man. He should have lived a long time. It would have been a good life for Stalyk and Marian.

Stalyk died an innocent man. A street battle between Roman soldiers and Zealot guerilla fighters caught him. He was killed just down the street from his home by an errant Roman arrow.

When Stalyk died, Marian began her daily routine. She survived as best she could. The world, long before the coming of Equal Rights, was not good to her.

Long before society freed women from chattel -- some say cattle -- status, life was not easy. Marian barely made her way in a cruel society. The nation held a trap for widows and women driven out by their husbands. Many found refuge in the life of a prostitute or slave to survive.

Not Marian.

Marian learned the sandal trade from Stalyk as they had worked together in the shop. Marian learned to cut and sew leather. She learned to work leather just right to be supple and soft. It must not rub blisters on working feet.

Stalyk's death forced Marian to carry on the business alone. This was difficult. The leather sellers in the market expected her to be weak-willed. She should be incapable of sharp trading. Sometimes they refused to bargain with her for the top quality skins. Some made a point of attempting to force the lesser quality of skin on Marian. Some demanded a high price for their own shoddy material and handiwork.

Sometimes friends gave her bits and pieces of leather to use. Most of her neighbors and relatives depended on her for their own sandal work. She never made much money.

Each day she was up before dawn making her little meals for the day. Some bread, a little fish and meal. On some celebration she might have a chicken or a piece of lamb or mutton.

Then she was at the market. Marian persistently showed her handmade sandals to potential customers. She had her knife and needles with her. With those tools, she could make on-the-spot repairs for waiting customers. Someone was always eager to have their sandals repaired. Her skill was all that protected their own tender feet.

Otherwise, the burning sand and rough stone of Jerusalem streets would tear feet apart.

Most of Marian's customers paid her in the time-honored way of all the world. Few had cash, so the exchange was in trade, in barter. Some had flour. Others had fish. Some had wood or metal or jewels. Some even had money.

Marian knew the money was most precious. It could purchase almost anything. It could go for services such as doctors or food. The coin could pay the entertainers that set up shop around the town at night. Silver or gold could buy perfume, or jewels. She could hold it for the days Marian did not feel well enough to work.

Money had another value in Marian's life. Since the street fight killed Stalyk, many things troubled Marian. She saw the Roman soldiers come and go. She heard of the constant fights with the guerrillas who came in off the desert. They irritated the Roman garrison, then ran back into the hills.

Marian saw death and destruction in the streets. Families broke up over wine-drinking. Men and women and children wandered homelessly along the streets. No shelter gave them sanctuary from the cold.

Marian felt hunger in her own body. She knew the fragility of her own existence. Any day might see her raped or ill or homeless.

If Rome should attack the population of the city, she was as defenseless as any. She saw the real possibility of her whole world coming to pieces around her. Any emergency might be her last.

Marian did not know that almost forty years later, Rome would sack the city. The government tried then to destroy the Jewish heritage. She could not have seen that, ninety years later, the Romans would exact bloody revenge. They would pull the beautiful rebuilt temple down. The roof and columns crushed several hundred men, women and children who had taken refuge there. She could not have known, but she could feel it coming.

This widow was not without strength. With the death of Stalyk, Marian had to find a new way. She committed herself to finding strength in one place, in one relationship.

Marian knew she needed to find just one anchor, one rock to stand firm. If she did, she could probably cope with anything the world might throw at her. Marian most needed that solid rock as a foundation.

She found her rock. The Lord, the ancient god of the Hebrew people, was her foundation. Her rock was present in Sinai and in Babylon. The rock was later at Auschwitz and Flossenberg, Gaza and Tel Aviv. This was her rock, her strength.

For twelve years, Marian made the trek to the temple

for her rock. She went to the sanctuary of Yahweh, the Lord. She spoke with the god whose name she knew. "I will risk my very existence for every moment of your life!"

For twelve long years she brought everything to the house of the Lord. Everything left at the end of the day came to the Lord. She held nothing back.

Sometimes it was a few coins. Often it was some gift. Sometimes it was flour, or a pair of children's sandals or other small item. She placed on a charity table. The poorest of the poor could help themselves here. Always it was a gift of everything she could put together now.

Then Marian went to a small corner for a long period in prayer. Each day the prayer was much the same as the day before.

"Blessed art thou, O Lord, ruler of the universe. Because you walk hand in hand with me through this day, I fear no evil. Your presence is a comfort to me. I bring this small bit you might use."

"For the sake of all who need your presence, establish on earth your kingdom among all of us. I thank you, Lord, that I might share in your presence with this gift. Amen."

With that gift, Marian became one with the will of the Lord. Marian's mission and the mission of her creator became one. The son of the Lord one day shared his life with her. Now she shared her life with the Lord.

Often Marian stayed, kneeling in the corner. She listened intently for the voice from the Lord. She often heard it rising through the sense and peace of the presence.

Then Marian began her walk back home. As she walked, she began to plan her work for later in the day. She had sandals to repair, leather to work, meal to grind, clothes to wash. Each day was much the same.

Jesus, watching this, spoke with conviction. "Truly I tell you. This poor widow serves the Lord. She has put in more than all the wealthiest of the nations together. They have contributed out of their abundance. This woman, giving out of her poverty, has put in all the living she had. The Lord will reward her."

Jesus knew her heart. He talked then about the problems of this life. He talked about the certainty of cities being places of destruction and desolation to the poor.

"In the midst of all this sorrow, have hope. When the world seems to come unglued in your very presence, lift up your hearts. It is in the midst of that hurt your redemption comes. It is in the midst of turmoil The Lord will save the people."

"When you see the destruction, you will know the Father is at work among you. The church will be there, clear to the end of all things. It must live. It must build, redeem, empower, chasten. My church must live."

Somewhere, someplace, the words of Isaiah rang again loud and clear. Jesus read them two years and a hundred and fifty miles away. Now he sang them again for all the world to hear.

"The spirit of the Lord is upon me. The Lord has anointed me to preach good news to the poor. He has sent me to proclaim release to the captives. I have come so the blind may recover their sight. I am here to free the oppressed. The Lord has called me to proclaim the acceptable year of the Lord."

# 53. Bittersweet Life
## Mark 13
### Rebuilding the Great Temple
### Gospel Time:485

"Oh! I hope he is right! Olman whispered only to himself as Jesus spoke to the small crowd at the temple garden."

Olman stood quietly while Jesus finished his condemnation of the majestic rebuilt temple. This man's words and Olman's thoughts were both blasphemous and treasonous. Imagine the scandal! The man said the new temple would come down yet again!

Millions of Jesus' time prayed for such an event. Still, to be heard saying this was an invitation to a flogging or even death. The great building was to be Herod's legacy to the holy city, Jerusalem. It would be a great legacy in the eyes of the whole world.

Not even the great buildings left by Solomon could eclipse the wonder of the great temple. It was the centerpiece of the throbbing heart in the sacred city, Jerusalem.

Millions of faithful Jews and wandering tourists at one time strolled through Solomon's temple every day or knelt in prayer. Even more came to see the remains of the temple built by the exiles returned from Babylon. Eventually the building collapsed from disuse after many years. But the curious and faithful still came.

The new temple was very different. Very different. The stones which the workers laid on top of each other were the size of large chariots. These monster stones required hundreds of men to move them. They had to move to carefully planned positions.

These stones were so large they could not possibly fall from their perches on top of one another. Herod and his architects planned things that way all along. The stones were so massive they just could move by accident.

The timbers for the roofs would require an entire city of men and women to roll them off their perches. Stealth could not move the timbers. The massive number of people involved in hoisting them along made quiet work impossible. Even an earthquake would find it hard to rattle the beams out from under their load.

Herod's people knew the Jews would celebrate that catastrophe if it came to the beautiful new temple. The Herodians were the most hated people. They required the mercenary armies of Herod as well as the legions of Rome to protect the pupped government.

But in spite of this rebellion, Herod pushed ahead with the temple. It was to be his monument to himself as much as a central structure of the Jewish people. Even the prayers of the faithful Jews in and for the temple would be part of Herod's monument to himself.

Herod knew he could eventually go to his grave feeling the positive opinions of Jews everywhere. In Jerusalem, Alexandria, Capernaum, Damascus, Athens and every place in between, he would die a hero. This much of Herod's legacy would be secure with the completion of the temple. This ego infuriated Olman now!

At one time, not many months ago, Olman worked hard. He would have gladly given hours of every day to rebuild the temple gladly. He knew about cutting stone and shaping timbers. His years of work gave him necessary experience now drilling the massive stones in the quarries.

Olman knew how to follow the almost imperceptible contours in the grain of the stone. With this knowledge he made them crack under stress. Drilling, shaping and smoothing with simple hand tools was not easy. It was possible now, and that was good.

Then Olman made a fateful decision. Many centuries past, his ancestors were deep within the priestly core of Hebrew faith. Then, like so many, the leaders and powers of the Hebrew people trekked off to the east as slaves. Olman's ancestors were part of the trek.

Even the great priest, Ezekiel, sprang from Olman's family line after a few years of captivity. Ezekiel worked hard to help the Hebrews keep a strong faith while in captivity in Abraham's ancestral homeland. He recalled and re-interpreted the ancient laws and customs of the people. He led their worship and their re-civilization as a people. It was not the Lord's will to live as a slave. A slave among the ziggurats and hanging gardens of Babylon and old Assyria must follow the will of the Lord..

Ezekiel lifted up the dreams and visions of his people. He taught them to use the great old themes in their worship and prayers. He gave them a promise of return to the land of their own people.

But when their family returned to Judah, they left behind their leadership and knowledge of temple ways. The men found their ways into the quarries where they mastered the art and science of cutting stone. The great new buildings around Jerusalem called for huge volumes of stone.

Olman knew himself to be an expert at cutting building stones. He could work as fast as anyone. He could also get the most production out of all his workers. Olman and his crew were simply the best at what they did.

Herod's architects and engineers began to see Olman as deserving to work up the ladder of success. He built himself a better home. He and his family wore better clothes. That is, for a time.

But Olman began to change. Surely, he worked his crew to cut the best stone from the quarry for the temple. But even in this Olman saw things in a new way.

He felt himself torn by the realities of temple life. Often Olman lay awake at night struggling with his own feelings. On the one hand, Olman and his crews were people of faith. Most of them were volunteers coming from Jerusalem or from far away places in pursuit of living relationships with Yahweh.

These faithful workers came believing and feeling that their time was faithful work. The time of drilling or cracking or trimming or moving the blocks would help them in their faith.

The volunteers were not blind to the hard work in the quarries or at the temple. Not at all! There would be blisters and pinched hands and fingers. Perhaps there would be broken arms or legs.

But these Hebrews kept coming in faith for the work in the quarries. They had been coming now for forty years.

Nor were they unaware that they might not return home at the close of a day or a month. A year of working to raise the walls a few inches might be their cause. Olman knew these struggles. However Olman believed serving through these hardships would help his faith grow.

Even the few who were forced into the labor as slaves found the numinous character of the temple itself. The work which went with it made one a little stronger.

There is something about the presence of Yahweh, the Lord of Israel, that made even slave life a little easier.

It is true. Most of them would have spent all day building the temple and all night tearing it down. But this was a temple of the Lord, above all things.

Even Olman felt some of this slave effect as he worked. He wanted the temple built. Olman wanted the temple to be the most magnificent building between Alexandria and Babylon. Yet he wanted to later tear down every stone he laid on top of another. He along those majestic porches and walls and columns. Olman knew why these stones had to come down.

The second major feeling in the heart of Olman came from his ancestral family. It came from his sense of living as a priest of the faith. His roots of priestly heritage traced back through Ezekiel and Isaiah and Levi and Abraham. Now the shadow of all these generations of Abraham bore a new witness. Trying to live as faithful priests came to a head in service to the temple. That shadow pulled on him as he laid stone upon stone for the new temple.

This new temple, in all its magnificence and glory, reminded Olman of a monstrous hurt. Herod's ancestors related more closely to the old enemies of Israel than to the generations of Abraham. They intended the temple as a showpiece for this hated foreigner on David's throne. It was only an afterthought to be a work of faith. Then it could be a religious icon for thousands of anonymous but spiritually and ethically minded Jews.

Olman found himself torn between the two sides. Every day which went by found him struggling more with his own feelings. His soul dueled with itself as a skilled craftsman and a faithful Jewish priest. To be certain, as both a Jew and a priest, Olman was happy as both a Jew and a priest. Olman was happy to live in the cushy surroundings of Herod's monument to himself.

Olman just wanted a great temple for the Lord. But as both a craftsman and a priest, Olman was something of a perfectionist. He wanted everything to be just perfect. Every extra crack in a stone; every hammer blow that left a dent in one of the massive oak timbers; was a bit of embarrassment to himself in front of the Lord and in his own eyes.

But each day, as the temple grew toward the vault of the sky, Olman questioned his actions more and more. He wondered about his own contribution to this monument to the hated Idumean king and his hand-picked high priest. He began to open up to his wife about his confused feelings toward his work and his heritage.

Now, Elena was not quite as torn about his work and about building the temple as was Olman. Oh, she lived with the struggle on a daily basis, just as did Olman. It was not such a personal issue for Elena. Rather, it was a problem for her because it tore Olman apart as he tried to work out his own faith. Even his own calling and his marriage were doubtful in his heart, and in hers.

The only way Elena could help, really, was to just listen to Olman's personal turbulence.. She could let him know she heard the cries of his heart. And she could pray.

One day, in the fortieth year of building the great temple, Olman left quietly in the early light. The supervisor of skilled workers told Elena he would be in the great temple all day. The crews had brought another slab for the temple from the quarried just outside Jerusalem.

Today was the day to place it in just the right spot. It was Olman's job to make certain it was placed in just the right position without damaging or cracking. As his crews worked, Olman became aware of a group of men and women gathered just a few feet away.

They were obviously looking at the temple with the same eyes as did Olman. The craftsmanship and engineering of the project fascinated them as they watched the temple grow. Block by block, shim by shim, the size, beauty and strength of the rebuilding project took shape. The vision of the new temple fascinated all the worshipers and tourists who came to Jerusalem.

But these pilgrims, too, had their doubts. Olman knew

by their clothing and their language they were pilgrims from Galilee. This made him glad they came all this distance to view his work. It also made him a little apprehensive. He knew the history of the mountain people of Galilee.

Many of the mountain people came from the north. They were followers of the ancient non-priestly prophetic group who called themselves the Sons and Daughters of Korah. They demanded absolute righteousness on the part of the Levitic priesthood.

The group were at least spiritual descendants of Korah. With his sons, he and his supporters died when they challenged the tyrannical rights of Moses and Aaron. These two demanded obedience of the Hebrews to their command.

The torah records Korah and his sons died at the hand of Yahweh. However, all of Galilee knew this was a euphemism for being slain by Moses, Aaron and their henchmen.

This action meant centuries of trouble for the hill people. Now Olman could only hold his peace. He could pray these men from Galilee would not start trouble by demanding righteousness at the newly rebuilt temple.

However, this was also an opportunity to talk with the visitors. As an old worker and an overseer nearing retirement, Olman had special privileges. He could take a few minutes to say "Hello" to visitors.

So he approached the group intending to speak at least to their leader. This man was talking as he watched Olman's crew into position. Olman heard the man speak words heard almost every day around the nearly completed temple.

"Do you see these great buildings here? Notice how difficult it is to place the stones in just the right way? Placing them just so requires the work of many men working together in just the right way to get the stones into their position. The building will be beautiful when it is complete."

Olman started to speak up to introduce himself. Thankfully, he waited another moment. He now said words as filled with blasphemy here as in any court in the land. Especially so in Jerusalem. They probably would have counted as treason anywhere.

It was an ancient curse against Jerusalem and the temple of Yahweh often spoken by the sons of Korah. "Listen carefully, my children! There will soon come a day when the Lord will throw down every one of these stones. Not one of these stones will stand atop another."

Olman's face turned white against these words. He knew the direction this diatribe was headed. It was spoken in the shadow of the great newly rebuilt temple. Then the pilgrim added the most puzzling words.

"After three days, the Lord will raise up another temple. Another temple, more holy than this, will raise up without the use of hands."

Instantly Olman's eyes and the eyes of the pilgrim locked together. In that distant embrace, Olman knew the meaning of the puzzling promise. "Another temple will raise up without hands."

This, too, was an ancient prophecy of the hill people of Galilee. It referred to the true certainty that the true temple was in the hearts of the people. It said that every person was the priest of their own temple. The Lord demands righteousness of every priest.

Olman could only nod his assent. Jesus, too, nodded with a little smile. Then he looked away.

Some of the others began to question him about his words. "And Jesus said, 'Let's go out to the Mount of Olives for some lunch. We will talk more about what we have seen."

As the pilgrim and his people went on around the beautiful temple, Olman returned to his crew. He was not certain the meaning of the prophecy for his own life. He knew only that these few simple words from a prophetic pilgrim at the temple his life changed his whole life. Yet they came from a simple man from the hill country of Galilee.

# 57. Words of Fire

Mark 11:1-11; Matthew 21:10-17; Luke 19:45-46
Psalm 118:1-2; 19-29; Isaiah 50:4-9a; Philippians 2:5-11
Geminel watches Jesus clean out the temple.
Sunday before Easter   Gospel Time: 490

Geminel stood before the altar of the temple. Absently, he watched the fire rise and fall there. The men of Israel gently laid their living sacrifices in the hands of the priests. The priest held the responsibility of the last moments of the sacrifices. The priests said the gentle prayers, then killed the sacrifices. After he cut them open, he laid them on the altar fire. There the fire consumed them.

These priests handling these duties worked with a deep reverence and respect. They were selected from their own communities as a matter of honor. The temple called them to serve only a few times in a lifetime of service.

Out in the courtyard the scene was quite different. Far less reverence and respect were evident there. More harsh reality appeared among those who sold sacrifices and keepsakes to the pilgrims.

"Get your sacrifices here! Get your doves, two spotless doves for twenty-five dollars. I just brought these in this morning. My boys have been raising them for pets.

Guaranteed no blemishes!"

"A-number one ram here for the sacrifice, only five hundred dollars!"

The prices asked for the sacrifices by those who bought and sold there shocked Geminel. Almost too much money changed hands. How could it be theologically correct? Must the proper sacrifice to the Lord operate on a cash basis only?

Geminel himself did as most of the poorer pigeon vendors did to get their pigeons. He went out at night into the city, hunting. By the light of the moon he caught two pigeons sitting on their roosts.

By faint lamplight, Geminel hurriedly inspected them for flaws. This pair looked all right. He could feel or see no broken wings or legs. The feathers were in good shape. Best of all, they were free. That was most important.

Now, with daylight, came the morning business. Men and boys brought more pigeons to sell. Geminel saw them out scouring the town for roosting pigeons last night. Now they brought in their unfortunate captives. The trappers sold them at the temple for outrageous prices.

The people who raised pigeons for profit commanded huge prices for the birds. They invested time and feed in the birds. The pigeon people raised the birds for profit. They could sell spotless birds to the wealthiest pilgrims for good money.

The scavengers, though, had little investment. Only a few minutes grabbing the birds from the roosts marked their commitment. These were the traders who ripped off the poorer pilgrims and the less devout. Many of these latter travelers came long distances. They walked or rode from as far as Spain, India, or Russia. Offering sacrifices at the temple was a major effort.

Now the climax of their journey came to them. Their own fatigue brought a clumsiness. The high pressure tactics of the traders took many of them in. The nature of the market made less than perfect animals bring high prices.

The priests, aware of the problems, generally looked the other way. All agreed embarrassing a traveler had no value to the resources of the temple. That traveler might not be particularly friendly to a supplier of shoddy products. No one wanted trouble here.

Geminel knelt in prayer at the temple steps. He tried to avoid the hubbub around him. Faithful Geminel concentrated on his prayer to the Lord. He vowed purity in his heart and commitment to the Messiah. Then Geminel rose in his turn. He stood in the line to watch a priest work. The priest took the two pigeons in hand while whispering a gentle prayer. The priest looked them over very carefully to be sure of their perfection. Then he ritually slaughtered them on the huge altar. After carefully inspecting their insides, the priest burned them as an offering to the Lord.

The flames rose and fell as they consumed the sacrifices. Occasionally a priest added wood brought by faithful pilgrims from their homes. Temple workers brought some wood from forests of the nation.

Geminel looked around at all those who were in the temple with him. Dozens of people gathered for the sacred rituals. Some came as priests. Some came as worshipers. Others arrived with hope to make money. Some wished to relieve boredom. A few came to bargain with the Lord for health or wealth or safety.

Everyone there hoped to profit somehow from something that might happen at the temple. The profit might be money for the traders or for the priests. It might be some better gift from the Lord for the worshiper. It might be just some excitement in life. If one looked, something could be found for almost everyone.

Some were wealthy or tried to pretend they were. Some were poor, or tried to convince the thieves they were. Geminel felt nothing but pity for the truly poor. Pity because it seemed they were truly hungry. Pity because they seemed out of place in the hubbub of buying and selling. This confusion went on as they offered up their sorry little gifts.

Geminel's mind wandered as he waited in line. His mind's eye pictured the man who controlled all this. One priest made things happen in the land.

This man in Geminel's thoughts was not the high priest. The high priest was just a functionary named by a ruling foreigner, Herod. The job of the high priest was to organize the religious work. It was not up to him to build the faith. It was not for him to run the nation and offer the sacrifices.

The Governor named the high priest. He was the one who made things happen around here. Right now, most of what was happening was bad.

Pilate was not really a military man, but he prided himself on his army. After all, it was the strongest force around. He had thousands of men who were well armed. Pilate equipped his people with the latest weapons made with the strongest bronze and iron.

Geminel had to chuckle at the image of Pilate's army as a sign of strength. Armies are not of strength but of weakness. Strong leaders and diplomats do not need armies for fighting battles within their nations.

We build strong nations on trust and honor, not on swords and spears. Pilate could not see that. He believed all the hype about the need for spears and machines and spies.

Pilate only used the temple to build his forced dictatorship. He needed protection only from those who questioned his dictatorship over their lives.

The temple was a good organization to protect the interests of Pilate's rule. All Pilate had to do was pass the word. One priest or another could call judgement. Those who were revolutionary enough to speak of a better way were in deep danger. The priest could call them radicals. He could use words like "bleeding heart liberals." He could use any words he could find.

Forget their concern came from reading the prophets of ancient Israel. Forget their compassion, their sense of justice. If they challenge the system, they are wrong.

These matters were no concern to Geminel. Geminel only wanted to stand before the Lord to make the sacrifice. Geminel wanted and needed to make peace with the Lord.

While Geminel waited, he wondered how the proceeds of this scene entered a priestly pocket. Finding out only cost Geminel a few coins into the hand of the officiating priest. As he waited in line, a ruckus began on the steps of the temple.

From where Geminel stood, he could not see what was happening. He could hear men shouting and see pigeons flying off. He could hear sheep bawling. Geminel was not really concerned until the temple guards buckled on their breastplates. Grabbing their shields as they ran, the guards were ready for battle.

Then a man whom Geminel had not seen before pushed his way through the crowd. Showing remarkable purpose, he came to the altar. There he knelt, obviously in deep and fervent prayer.

While he knelt, a silence filled the temple. The whole world seemed to come to a complete stop. No one moved.

Fifty temple guards seemed frozen. The priests stopped their sacrificial slaughter momentarily. Their hands lifted slightly, poised with sharp knives, not moving. The milling crowd paused as if waiting for something extraordinary to happen.

When the strange man rose the holy room was quiet. One wealthy man in the line walked over to the stranger. The stranger stood as the man whispered something in his ear. The quiet stranger listened to the Pharisee, then slowly lifted his eyes.

He could see the men in the temple, going about their daily work. The rich and poor, hometowners and wanderers waited while he surveyed the scene.

Jesus looked out through the door of the temple at the hovels of the poor. The poor were forced to build outside the city walls. They lived without water and without the protection of the walls. These poor could only dream.

Strong eyes filled with tears as he saw the broken down shacks of the poor. The hovels pushed up against the outside walls of the city.

Inside the walls, the homes of the wealthy stood as fortresses. They were vaults for the wealth of the nation.

He spoke. "Go tell Herod, that sly fox, the son of man is here. Tell him I will heal the sick for a couple days. I will be giving hope to the poor. I will be making the blind see, and releasing the captives of a sick world."

"This city, Jerusalem, the city of David, has had its chance. How often the poor of the city came to you in the Lord's temple. How often have those of my people come to you in their need? My people live in those mud huts in filth and in disease and in hunger. They have asked repeatedly for help. You could have taken them in as a mother hen covers her chicks. Yet you did not."

"Instead, you stoned the prophets. You murdered those who told the truth about you. You trampled the poor in your search for the almighty gold."

"Jerusalem, they will destroy you. They will not just circumcise you. They will clean cut you off."

Jesus paused a moment. "I will go away now, but I will be back. When I return you will say `Hosanna! Blessed is he who comes in the Name of the Lord!'"

As the man left, Geminel knew the Galilean would be back. More trouble would come -- lots more trouble. Geminel knew Herod's soldiers would be waiting for the man. He stirred huge waves in the human sea called

Israel. Geminel knew the temple guards were ready to fight against the man. He had told the truth about the city and the temple and the priests.

Somehow, Geminel knew down deep inside this man was no loser.

All the armies of the nations did not destroy this ordinary man of the world. A hundred elite temple guards could not hold him. The self-righteous statements and the patriotism of the wealthy could not block his intent. They did not hold back the forces this man loosed. The class system that made up the nation could not withstand his justice.

This man came back, all right. He came back to stay.

# 58. Thirty Coins
## Mark 14
### What could Judas have been thinking?
### Holy Week   Gospel Time: 500

The small bag he carried was nearly empty now. The long, steady walk through along the international trade route cost nearly the entire financial resource of Jesus' group. From Capernaum to Jerusalem, Jesus seemed to find a route which passed through every tiny village and major city. Bethsaida, Scythopolis, Samaria, Jericho and so many others became stopping points for this pilgrimage. Every cluster of five or six houses seemed to cry out for the disciples to take a few hours' rest.

Every rest stop found a little more of the precious reserve of the disciples staying behind when the group left. Some small coin often stayed in the pocket of a food vendor at the village market. Occasionally they treated Jesus and the others to fruit, bread and wine by villagers. They would do anything to convince Jesus to stop and stay. They were eager to listen to his prophecies and feel his healing.

A few of the more serious faithful, especially in small villages and hamlets along the road, insisted on giving money. These people seemed caught up in Jesus' call for the purification of the temple. His words were a commanding issue during the reconstruction under Herod. Many wanted to support any movement to straighten out the mess and the temple. They particularly wanted to help. If they had any sense they would drive Herod from the throne of their Promised land, they would help. So they chose to put their money in the hands of the man who might do the job. He appeared to be going to Jerusalem to drive Herod and his chief priest from the temple.

Now that Jesus found his way to Jerusalem, money was even more difficult to find. News travels fast. As Jesus traveled south from Capernaum, villagers heard of his coming several days before he arrived. The first disciples showed up early to arrange for food and shelter. Then when Jesus arrived, a crowd quickly gathered to witness the event.

Some people touched his robes, hoping for a miracle. The blind hoped to see. The lame hoped to walk.

Others just wanted to judge for themselves this man, Jesus. They needed to know if he was some sort of scam artist. Was he just a misguided man from the northern hill country, a lunatic or a true prophet?

Anyway, whenever a crowd showed up, someone usually had food to share or sell. Someone else brought wine. Always, bread was available.

Now in Jerusalem, everything cost money. Bread, wine, fish, meat. Money. Money. Money. Judas found himself worrying more and more over the quickly dwindling resources he held in his leather bag.

This leather bag was a gift from his brother, Hiram. Hiram worked leather at his home in Capernaum. When he heard Jesus asked Judas to handle the small treasure for the group, Hiram was happy. He felt good about Judas' new responsibility. He was eager to be supportive. So Hiram handed Judas this bag. It had a long leather drawstring which looped around Judas' neck and waist to hold it close to his body.

The bag never held much money. The disciples rarely had more than a few coins between them. Now, as they visited Jerusalem and Bethany for a few days, even those few coins were disappearing rapidly. Judas knew they were in trouble. Begging for coins for the purification of the temple did not seem to fit.

So Judas kept Jesus informed about what was happening to the money. To Judas, it seemed that Jesus was very interested to know the status of the small treasury. It was almost as if Jesus tried to schedule their expenses. He seemed to want to hold only enough money to last through the Passover Seder. At least, as Judas carefully pinched the budget, it seemed that would be the case for the treasury.

On the day of Passover, the disciples all rose early. This was a great holy day for Jews around the world. From the original Passover until the day Jesus worshiped at the temple, Passover has been part of Hebrew life.

Today was special, even for a Passover. It was the first time all the disciples spent the day together in the company of Jesus. It was the first Passover the disciples and the others in the group came to the temple with Jesus.

The talk of the group that morning involved an unspoken question. Would this be the day Jesus would purify the temple? If so, how would he do it? Obviously the disciples and the others should help, but how? Would Jesus hold a special ceremony in the temple? The disciples all had so many questions they could not ask.

After the morning meal of bread and fruit, Peter and John came to Jesus with a simple problem. These two trusted leaders often helped organize things. Finding food or shelter always took time and effort. In this, they regularly found themselves talking with Judas about the status of the treasury. Today, Peter and John asked Judas for enough money to purchase supplies for the Seder.

The supplies needed were simple. Some simple flat bread, some dark wine, some maror which tastes much like horseradish. They needed some charoses, a sweet mixture of fruit, wine, nuts and spices. Some hyssop, parsley or another simple green garnish would serve.

Above all, they must slaughter properly and prepare the lamb according to Jewish law. For a family, or in a very poor community, they could provide a proper substitute for the lamb. The most proper substitute for the Passover lamb was a chicken neck, cooked and ready to serve.

Today there could be no substitute. This was the day the disciples and the others felt was the first day of the purification of the temple. This day, this meal, was just too important in the history of the world. Peter and John knew no substitute was possible now for the lamb. Not today.

So Peter spoke openly to Jesus. "Jesus, today is the Passover, as you know. We have already talked about that. We want to get ready for the Seder. Judas says we have just enough money for everything, including a healthy yearling lamb."

Jesus smiled at this. He always seemed happy when food enough for everyone, including himself, was near.

Peter continued. "We still have a problem, Jesus. Maybe you have an answer. Just where shall we prepare our meal?"

Peter was right. Jesus did have an answer. "Go to the market in the city. A man who knows you will meet you and give you a sign. He will be carrying a large jug of water on his right shoulder. Ask him where we can celebrate the Passover. Tell him 'The teacher needs a room for the Seder.' Then follow him."

When Jesus finished asking his people to do something, he just stopped. He had a way of letting them know he felt he had said all he needed to say. Peter and John had already figured the cost of the meal. The largest expense would be the lamb. Now Judas emptied the contents of the little leather bag into John's hand.

John quickly checked the few coins. Yes, enough food for the meal was at hand. John gave coins to several disciples and the women to use to purchase the supplies. John gave the coins for the lamb back to Judas. Judas and Thomas would locate and slaughter the lamb, then roast it. The others were to go into the market and buy their needs for the Seder. Then the group would bring their material back, and wait.

Peter and John, Thomas and Judas left at that point. Jesus seemed to want to rest before evening, so he found a soft pallet for a bed. Others did the same, until the room was quiet. Most slept, but three or four sat in a corner and talked quietly among themselves.

Peter, John and Judas talked as they walked toward the meeting place. Jesus must have arranged this meeting in the last day or so. He often just left the group for days or hours at a time. The disciples felt he had a purpose for each absence, so they did not really ask.

They had no concern about the man who was to meet

them in the city. If he was carrying a large jug of water on his shoulder, he obviously was an innkeeper. No man, other than an innkeeper, carried a large jug of water. A single man might carry a small jug. A man with a disabled wife might carry a jug. A married man with a healthy wife would not. Either his wife or a servant would carry the water.

Being an innkeeper, the man would have a room fit for the Passover. The room could accommodate about twenty people for the Seder. He also would have an oven to roast the lamb. The oven would be hot today as the innkeeper's wife prepared the general evening meal.

The three men stepped into the marketplace and stopped. How could they find the messenger?

The four did not need to worry. Shortly after they stepped into the marketplace, a man carrying a large jug of water stepped in front of them. "Are you looking for a room?"

Peter answered. "The teacher needs a room for the Passover." The man with the jug mad no sound. He simply nodded and turned away. The others followed as he led them to the upper room.

As they approached the inn, Thomas and Judas left the others on their own mission. They had a lamb to find.

Back to the market they went. It was now late in the morning, and the lamb must be roasting soon. They found a lamb they felt was satisfactory. Then they slaughtered and dressed it according to Jewish law. The skin was left for the vendor as part of the purchase agreement.

Thomas left with the lamb. He had to get the lamb in the oven when possible. It needed to be roasted in a gentle heat so it would not over-cook.

Judas told Thomas he wanted to stop by the temple for a moment of prayer. Judas would be back to the room for the meal in a few minutes. Then he would go bring the others to the inn. He made his way to the temple. Inside, he found a couple priests waiting for their own Seder to begin.

Judas approached them boldly. "Holy men, I have heard some of you might like to meet Jesus, the miracle man from Galilee. I believe I can arrange an introduction , if anyone is interested."

One priest left immediately. He went to a back room of the temple. There, he explained the situation. A much higher ranking priest came out to talk with Judas. "I would like to meet this Jesus. I am really interested. Why do you want to do this for us?"

Judas did not pause. "For money. We need money for food and shelter. I am certain we will be going back to Galilee soon. For money. In advance."

The priest paused. "OK. Thirty silver coins. No more."

Judas' mouth fairly watered at this. No more empty

leather purse. Some weight in the coin bag hanging around his neck. He nodded. Another priest immediately went to the back room. He re-appeared soon with a coin bag. Then he counted thirty silver coins into Judas' bag.

Judas told the priests where they could find him that evening. He knew Jesus would want to make his normal evening visit to the Mount of Olives. The priests should be ready, waiting near the Mount.

At some point, Judas would meet him and tell the messenger where to bring the others. There, he would greet Jesus with the usual greeting of the land, a kiss on each cheek. That would be the sign. From there on, the priests could make themselves known.

That was enough. Judas left, then, to make his way back to the others waiting for word. He led them to the inn for the Seder. While the others finished preparing the room for the special meal, Judas helped Thomas finish roasting the lamb. While the lamb cooked, the group made sure the room was clean. It had to be suitable for Jesus. After all, Jesus was the one to purify the temple and the people. His own life must be pure and holy.

That evening, after supper, Jesus and most of the disciples went along the street to the Mount of Olives. At the Mount of Olives, Jesus talked about his own life and ministry. He said that someone would betray him, and that others would turn away from him.

Of course, everyone denied the possibility. However, it was obvious to all that Jesus was well aware of all the talk that had gone on. He ended the evening by telling Judas to go quickly to do what he had to do.

Then Jesus led the group into the garden of Gethsemane to talk and pray. This was their custom, relaxing in conversation and prayer after a meal. After a time, Jesus went off into a corner of the garden by himself for his own time of prayer.

Judas watched all this silently for a time. Jesus so concentrated on his conversation with the Creator he did not notice what his disciples were doing. Judas slipped into the shadows, then out the gate to the street.

At the street, Judas saw a priest in the street, hiding in the shadows. Judas waved at the priest, and turned to walk back into the garden. Immediately the priest appeared through the gate with several other priests, a couple slaves, and several temple guards.

Judas walked to Jesus. He gave Jesus the old traditional greeting, then turned away. Immediately, the temple guards surrounded Jesus, tying his hands together.

Seeing what was happening, Thomas simply panicked. Jesus long-time friend and supporter drew his short sword quickly. He swung it at the slave of the high priest. His wild gesture only made a small cut on the man's ear.

Jesus told Thomas to put his sword away. Then he held

the slave's ear in his still-tied hands until the blood stopped flowing.

The guards, the priests and the slaves left the Garden of Gethsemane with Jesus. This bundle of power took him off to a fate none of the disciples could have believed possible. The Trial, the Cross, the Tomb, and the New Life.

## 59. Feast
John 13:1-35; Exodus 12:1-14;
Psalm 116:1-19; 1 Corinthians 11:23-26
The community gathers for Passover.
The Week before Easter    Gospel Time: 510

Thomas was so very close to Jesus. Other disciples said Thomas was a twin to Jesus. Thomas was always near, usually near enough to touch Jesus. Jesus spoke of Thomas from the cross to his mother. "Mother, your son."

Then Jesus spoke quietly to Thomas, "Your mother."

Thomas and Jesus, Jesus and Thomas. Quite a pair, these two from Nazareth. Where you saw one, you saw the other. Many who knew them well assumed they were at least brothers.

Thomas was the passionately committed disciple. When Jesus announced his mission, it took only a few seconds for Thomas to choose. He instantly committed his life to Jesus. For Thomas, the decision to adopt the mission of Jesus was not difficult.

Thomas was the first disciple to wave the palm branches and cry "Hosanna!" When Jesus asked for food for the crowds, it was Thomas who answered. He accepted without question the challenge of finding enough food for everyone. He just knew somehow enough food was on the table. Jesus said so. What Jesus said, Thomas believed. They were that way since childhood.

Tonight the Passover celebration in the little room ran its course. Thomas let every word and thought of the ancient ritual touch his soul. Jesus asked "Why on this night do we eat maror, the bitter herb?"

Thomas felt the pain of the old ones in slavery as James answered. The memory of slavery under Egyptian masters gnaws at the heart of every Hebrew. Thousands of years have not softened the pain.

In a dish by Jesus a bitter herb called maror called attention to itself. It tasted something like bitter horseradish. "We eat the maror to suffer again the pain of life in slavery. We had no life for ourselves. We could only make bricks for the homes and temples of the Egyptians."

James fervently intoned the words of harshness and truth. Judas Iscariot paid no heed to the emotions of the Seder. Judas had his own agenda for the evening hours.

Judas was not a Galilean. He had little thought for the ordinary dreams and plans of the other eleven. Fishing Lake Tiberias was alien to his personal world. Building boats, sewing sails and fashioning furniture were not his crafts. Judas was an organizer, a planner. He was even a schemer. He could make things happen.

Now on this holy night Judas was ready to make something happen. It must be something that changed the whole world. It was on his shoulders. Only this experienced organizer had the skill to string together events to fulfil Jesus' mission. Continual fishing and healing were not enough. They could not provide the whole impetus for the effect of Jesus' life. Judas was not satisfied.

As a power broker, Judas had a cloud of people around him. They either owed him something or wanted his favor. Judas could ask for a variety of help, and someone always answered.

The parade earlier in the day was a fine example of Judas' work. Judas recalled the traditional style of welcoming a prophet or a king. Drying palm fronds lay in the street. The crowd had cut and waved them for Jesus.

Spectators along the route had cried out "Hallelujah!" This old word took on the meaning "The Lord Comes!" Some persons even took off their cloaks to cover the paving stones.

Judas made all this come about. Passing the word and a few coins to his acquaintances was enough. By whispering a king was coming, he set the wheels in motion. This might even be the new king of the Jews. All

Judas had to do was whisper something to Thomas. He said Jesus looked the part of the "king of the Jews." Thomas took the cue. He grabbed a palm frond and shouted "Hallelujah! Hosanna!" Judas' plants did the rest. Nothing could hold them back now.

A crowd of pilgrims is easy to incite. These pilgrims had been on the road for weeks, months, even years. Inside these faithful hearts rose up an irresistible urge to shout and sing and laugh. They were looking for something to celebrate, something to shout about. After the long dusty road, they were ready. With a frond in the air, pilgrims felt the temptation to shout for joy. "Hallelujah!" The coronation by acclamation had begun hours ago. Now more work must be done.

In the dimly lit room Jesus asked the question. "On this night, why do we eat only unleavened bread?" Thomas listened carefully to Bartholomew's answer. The answer to this question was the most exciting moment in the passover seder.

Bartholomew, himself, could have talked for hours. The fear and haste as the Hebrews left Egypt lived on in the room. He could somehow make himself and the other witnesses feel the terror. The hot breath of the pursuing Egyptian soldiers seemed to come over them. Bartholomew spoke only a few words of the Seder. The disciples could almost hear the roar of Egyptian chariots.

The clank of swords and shields was very near. They could feel the dust in their eyes. The Lord's people fled across the desert in a panic. They did not take a moment to gather their belongings. Even grabbing a bit of leaven to make their bread rise would have been fatal. The remnants of the Lord's people had to run quickly for their very lives.

Thomas well knew the hurts of life. As a boy, Thomas knew so well the pain of rejection and failure. For some reason, he always believed himself to be different from the other boys. Perhaps being an orphan raised by his grandmother was a heavy load. Sometimes it seemed his mind worked a little slower than others. Sometimes his body just did not respond the way it should. He could not dance like other boys. He never won a race.

Thomas never had the funds the other boys had to spend on young women. All he could earn from his menial jobs and from begging went into staying alive. His clothes were rags. He made and remade his sandals and remade them again.

Deep inside, Thomas had the sense of the future. He knew one day life would be much better for him. The sturdy disciple did not know how it could happen. He just knew a better was ahead. His faith kept him constantly on the lookout for that sign, that presence. Thomas expected some omen to let him know he was turning his life around.

Now, Jesus led the Seder festival tonight. Thomas was sure this was the sign. Two weeks ago Thomas had been close when Jesus gave Blind Bart back his vision. When Jesus made it possible for a crippled man to walk, Thomas was there. Thomas had seen with his own eyes the response of thousands of people to Jesus. Jesus walked and talked easily among the crowd. They knew Jesus as a friend. Something of Jesus' character rubbed off on those around him and walked with him. He let them sense the power and truth of his presence. Oh, sure, some scoffed at these events. These were so few doubters as to be meaningless. One need not worry about the doubters.

Thomas felt much more with his heart than he saw with his eyes. He felt so good being close to Jesus in spirit and body. It had been that way between them since they were growing up together in Nazareth. Thomas watched and listened and tried to learn all he could. Thomas wanted to give up everything else to do what was right for this man. He chose to commit his life entirely to Jesus. Thomas' mission was to make Jesus' life as good as possible. Thomas had no concern for the cost to himself.

Thomas could see no point in a partial commitment. No honor is found in keeping one's fingers crossed. This was all or nothing. Was it a huge risk? Of course. Thomas had only enough personal strength of character left for one last try. He needed to make something of himself. Now was the critical time. If not now, he might as well go back to Galilee. He could spend his life dragging the fish nets across the Sea of Galilee.

Of course, Thomas was not the only one ready to commit his life. James, Peter, Judas, all the rest did as well. Everyone was ready to do whatever Jesus wanted or needed. If Jesus wanted to find a room to celebrate this meal, someone found it. When Jesus needed a donkey for some purpose, someone found it.

Thomas struggled with the depth of his own commitment to Jesus. Jesus took Judas aside and whispered to him. "Tell them I will be in the garden. Go quickly now." When Judas hesitated and seemed to protest, Jesus said again, "Go. Now. Do it now."

When Judas left the room his first steps took him to a wine maker knew. It was through Hallel Judas found the planted characters for the parade. They served to incite the crowd for Jesus earlier on the road. Now Judas knew whom he could trust.

Judas took two or three long dregs from one of Hallel's wineskins. He knew no other means to give himself courage. Then Hallel took Judas to a private room in the temple. Hallel knew several temple priests gathered there each evening. These busy men needed their own time of gossip, relaxation and beverage.

With only a few words, Judas arranged to lead the temple guards to Jesus. Judas told them where to find the house. He promised to give the guards a sign to show Jesus to them. The guards must be absolutely certain. Judas returned to the house, with the guards following close behind.

By the time Judas returned, Jesus had been in the garden close to an hour. All the intense emotions inside him seemed to come tumbling out. The disciples sat in little groups around the fringes of the open area. Some slept. Others talked quietly among themselves. All were intensely conscious of Jesus' presence and his prayer. However, none could look at him or speak to him. Nor did they know what to do for him.

The next hours were a time Thomas wanted to forget. Judas came quietly into the garden. He approached Jesus with arms open as if to give Jesus a hug. The guards seemed to appear without warning behind Judas.

When Peter saw the guards appear he realized immediately what was happening. He drew his own short sword and swung wildly at a guard. Peter made a nasty cut across the back of the guard's ear. Blood flowed wildly down the man's neck and onto the garden floor.

Seeing the flowing blood, Jesus took the guard's head in his hands. He pressed his fingers against the gash.

Jesus' own hands became red with the blood of the guard. Finally the blood stopped flowing.

The whole earth seemed silent while Jesus worked to stop the flow of blood. He did not move his hands for several seconds.

Then Jesus simply took his hands away from the head of the guard. As he lowered them to his side, he spoke quietly. "I am ready. Did you really have to come after me with spears and swords? Is my reputation really such that you were afraid for your lives?"

The guards tied Jesus' hands, then took Jesus back to the temple. There they turned him over to the chief priest. For the next few hours a circus of confusion reigned. Trial, gossip, fear and accusation took the Jerusalem stage. The priests took Jesus to Pilate, who sent him back. Both the priests and the government trumped up whatever charges they could think of. They wanted to kill him. Any reason would do. They tried him for blasphemy and treason, and hung him on the cross to die.

## 60. Where Are Your Friends?
### Mark 14:53-65; Psalm 62; 145
Why did Jesus' friends abandon him?
Gospel Time: 520

The hot, dusty roads took a little too long to cool down in the evening. The dust flew around sandals, mixing with sweat from calloused feed as they walked. After a couple hours walking in the early morning, feet just went along for the ride.

Usually, the men walked the road on the west side of the river in the afternoon. Sometimes, if the day was especially warm, they walked the road on the east side, out of the sun. It all just depended on the brightness of the sun and the hot air. They crossed the river easily at the many fords. After they crossed, the group could perhaps more easily walk in the shade of the trees along the river. The roads were not much more than trails along the shallow river. Caravans, troops and individuals moved along either bank as they chose.

As they walked, the men and women often formed and reformed small groups of two to six persons. For a time, the new groups walked and talked together. In this way they could share with each other their deepest concerns and cares. They were well aware of their target,

Jerusalem. Most of them had been to the great Holy City previously on a pilgrimage or on business.

They also could sometimes just walk along quietly, thinking of little but putting one foot in front of the other. Little pattern came to their movement. The only pattern an observer would have noted was the men often let Jesus walk alone. He seemed to want it that way.

Two of the followers often walked only a little distance away from Jesus. They seemed to want to give Jesus his privacy. However, they also chose to be close enough to display their faithfulness to their leader. Whenever one of them moved closer to Jesus, the other stayed just as close. Only when they agreed to back off did they give Jesus some privacy.

They spread the group sometimes out along the road from the Sea of Galilee to Jericho. A small group might be as much as a mile ahead of or behind Jesus and the main group. If they were ahead, they might stop and rest while the larger group caught. If they were behind, they might sometime walk a little faster to keep pace.

Jesus seemed to always walk at the same speed, at the front or the rear of the group. If the group chose to walk fast, Jesus was sometimes at the rear, alone. If the group dragged some, Jesus might be in the lead, either with his companions or not. He seemed to have his mind set on reaching Jerusalem at a certain time. Whether his people kept his timetable or not was their own problem.

Even the farms and small villages along the river allowed Jesus to follow a simple daily pattern. As Jesus approached a settlement, two or three of his group broke away to 'scope' things out. They usually went into the village, stopping only with the elders at the village gate. Their task was to tell them Jesus was coming near.

While some elders went into the village to spread the word, Jesus' people arranged for whatever they needed. If they approached the village at mealtime, they arranged for food and water and wine. Often the group had no need to purchase supplies. The presence of some ill or crippled person in town was a good thing, in some ways. Jesus' followers might mention that he had healed a similar case back in Capernaum. The townspeople would be familiar with that possibility. They brought out supplies of food, wine and water for the walkers from the land of sacred healers.

So Jesus healed wherever he sensed a need. Then he talked about his vision for the world, a vision of peace and wholeness. After a time, if some hours of walking time remained, the group walked on.

If no walking time remained in the day, the group simply settled down just out of town. Usually, inside or outside the main gate did not matter. After an evening of talking and snacking and bathing in the village pool, they talked openly with any who came. Then, sleeping until dawn came easily for the young crowd.

Then in the morning, after a time of prayer and a good breakfast of fruit and bread and fish or lamb, Jesus stood and simply began walking. South. Toward Jerusalem.

It was in these times Jesus felt strongest. His legs were fresh, his face was clean, and his belly was full.

In these times Jesus felt the most vulnerable. Often after he had walked a half-hour or so he looked around for the others. Sometimes he could see only one or two of the group straggling along, back a half-mile or so. Perhaps the others were still cleaning up their camp. They might be dealing with a late-comer who need a healing or some kind words.

Nevertheless, at these times, Jesus walked alone toward his fate in Jerusalem, at the call of the rebuilt temple. He wondered. What about his friends? Would they keep up with him to Jerusalem? To whatever came next?

As Jesus walked, he enjoyed remembering the old Psalms. They gave him great strength and comfort in his lonely hours along the road. Psalm 62 was one of his favorites as he walked.


For the Lord alone my soul waits in silence;
     from the Lord comes my salvation.
Yahweh alone is my rock and my salvation,

my fortress; they shall never shake me.
How long will you assail a person,
    will you lay siege to your victim, all of you,
    as you would a leaning wall, a tottering fence?
Their only plan is to throw down a person of prominence.
    They take pleasure in words not true;
  they bless with their mouths,
    but inwardly they curse.    Selah

Jesus know what was coming. Jesus knew, but James and John and Peter and Judas did not know. They did not know. They only walked the road to Jericho and to Jerusalem because Jesus walked. They chose to be with him. They chose to be companions.

After a time, Jesus and his people left Jericho. They left, walking slowly along the road to Jerusalem. The road was uphill the first half of the trek. Through a canyon, a wadi, where danger lurked at every moment.

The people stayed close along the Jericho road. Robbers or muggers or lions or dogs might attack stragglers, or those who go too far ahead. So through the wadis, the travelers stayed within thirty or forty yards of their leader as he walked steadily along.

As Jesus walked, he used the time to teach, and to prepare his people for their responsibilities as his disciples. He told parables as he walked. The two closest companions heard the story best. They listened for whatever meaning it had for themselves.

"Once a man walked this very road, going up from Jericho to Jerusalem. He went for trading and for a pilgrimage to the temple. As he walked lone, robbers attacked and beat him. They clubbed him and kicked him, and stole his money and his goods. Then they left him for dead."

"Soon a Levite came along. He saw the wounded man lying in the road and walked by on the other side."

"Then came a priest, on his way to offer sacrifices at the temple, as was his sacred duty. He, too, passed by on the other side of the road."

"Then a Samaritan came up the road. He attempted to get to Jerusalem to trade  and to visit the temple. He led a donkey loaded with valuable leathers and cloth and other good things for trading."

"The Samaritan saw the wounded man on the road, bleeding. He used some of his own clothing to bind up the wounds of the man. Then he loaded the man on his donkey, and led him back to Jericho to an inn. The Samaritan had stayed often at the inn."

"At the inn, the Samaritan paid the innkeeper to care for the wounded man and keep him for a month. He said, 'You care for him until he is ready to travel. If this money is not enough, I will pay the rest when I come through next month. You know I am good for the care.'"

"So, friends, what do you say? Who was doing the will of him who sent me? Who was the real friend to the wounded man?"

One disciple, it may have been Thomas, answered plainly. "Jesus, the one who bound up the wounds was the real friend. He proved it when he paid the innkeeper to care for the wounded man."

Jesus said, "Go, and do the same." The men could not have known of the wounds Jesus would suffer in a few days.

After some time, the temple guards arrested Jesus in Jerusalem. One man who walked closely with Jesus betrayed him to the temple guards who came to arrest him. The guards dragged him to a sham trial in front of the high priest. They tried to steal his manhood from him.

One who walked with Jesus tried to stay close enough to see what was happening. Someone accused him of being one of those who came to town with the group from Capernaum. "You are one of them! I know it. I have seen you walking close to him!"

The man who walked close to Jesus said, "You are wrong, man. I have never seen this fellow before. You must be dreaming. Or maybe you are drunk."

Then the guards stripped him and whipped him. All the while they taunted Jesus. "Where are your friends?

Where are those who were with you? Do they not care? Will they just let you die?"

Peter had followed him at a distance, right into the courtyard of the high priest. He was sitting with the guards, warming himself at the fire while they talked about this evil man, Jesus. Now the chief priests and the whole council were looking for testimony against Jesus to put him to death. They could find none, no testimony at all to use. Many gave testimony against him, but their testimony did not agree.

Some stood up and gave testimony against him. "We heard him say, 'I will destroy this temple made with hands.' He said, 'In three days I will build another, not made with hands.'" Herod's workers were rebuilding the temple. They had worked forty years to make it new again.

Even on this point their testimony did not agree. Then the high priest stood up before them. He said, "Jesus, have you no answer? What is it that they are saying against you?"

He was silent and did not answer. Again the high priest asked him, "Are you the Messiah, the Son of the Blessed One?"

Jesus said, "I am. You will see the Son of Man seated at the right hand of the Power. He will come with the clouds of heaven."

Then, Caiaphas, the high priest tore his clothes and said, "Why do we still need witnesses? You have heard his blasphemy! What is your decision?"

All of them condemned him as deserving death. Some began to spit on him, to blindfold him, and to hit him, saying to him, "Prophesy!" The guards also took him over and beat him.

Peter and some others remembered Jesus' parable, told to them along the Jericho road.

Amen.

# 61. Jubal's Timbers

Matthew 27:15-26; Mark 15:6-14;
Luke 23:6-25; John 18:1ff
Isaiah 52:13-53:12; Psalm 22; Hebrews 10:16-25
The temple carpenter supplies a cross.
Week Before Easter    Gospel Time: 530

Callouses on rough and weathered hands betray years of hard work and careful planning. Jubal tried hard to be an honest man. The community knew him as a faithful patriot and a man of the Lord. He tried to make an honest living from doing what he knew and loved. His passion was for the beautiful woodwork of the great temple of Jerusalem. Jubal felt the strength and unity of the holiest spot of the world.

Jubal also worked some for the Roman government, for the governor of Judea, in Jerusalem. This temple carpenter fixed roofs and repaired cabinets around the governor's palace. He built furniture, chairs and desks for the government offices in Jerusalem. Occasionally the governor needed something built that required the work of the most skilled artisan. Jubal repaired many pieces of furniture for the temple. Someone always called Jubal. He knew the wood best.

Such a faithful man of the Lord and descendant of

David's family was thoroughly indispensable. He fixed things around the temple. A door here, a drapery rod there. Sometimes he even made a bit of new covering for the roof. The Jews appreciated the faithfulness of his work and artistry. Even when the temple was no more, he was honored.

For all his public work, Jubal nearly always worked alone. Few people ever came into his little shop. Deep in the bowels of the governor's palace, the solitary room was his personal sanctuary. When they bothered him, they needed a specialist for something difficult. Something needed fixed or built by one who had a master craftsman's touch. As a master woodworker, Jubal could run things his own way in the quiet corner.

He prided himself on keeping things neat and orderly in the shop. Jubal worked there alone. He had no excuses. If he could not find a board or piece of hardware, he was responsible.

Jubal had many boards and rods stacked around his shop. His supplies waited for their own purposes. Every piece had its own character. Each bit of precious wood had its own personality, it seemed. A different feel, smell, and sight. The grain ran a little differently with each board, even out of the same tree. This gave each piece a special place in his heart.

His eye often wandered to two worn but well preserved

timbers. The waited assignment, stacked neatly along the wall. Jubal saved them for some special construction need. It must be very important, something only they could fulfill. Experience told him to keep them ready. Someday they would serve as part a new section of floor or roof some place. He might need them to brace up a ceiling somehow.

For whatever purpose might come, Jubal knew an eerie feeling inside him about these pieces. The timbers must be very strong and very straight if they were so important. So Jubal spent many hours with them. He sanded them smooth, dried them just so and oiled them just so. He did what he could to protect the posts from desert heat and dryness.

Jubal rescued these beams from a temple courtyard gate frame project. Herod's temple rebuilders were widening the frame so a government chariot could drive straight through. For faithful Jews, this was blasphemy. No chariot had ever been inside the courtyard for any reason. In recent times some priests saw a need to make it possible.

The big issue was the debate on the coming of the messiah. Promised for hundreds of years by Isaiah and others, it must be time. Some priests said when the messiah comes the Lord will provide signs. He will come in a chariot pulled by a team of great horses. This chariot, driver and rider should have clear path. They would carry the messiah to the inner chambers of the great temple.

Many priests disagreed with the action. However, the high priest, deep in his heart, looked for his own reward. Perhaps he knew the will of the messiah. The high priest recognized the nation might accord him the same privileges. He might even be chosen to be the driver of the messianic chariot. Perhaps he might just ride along, or stand on a second chariot. So the gate must be wider.

New posts were found for the wider gateway. Jubal fell heir to the old beams. Jubal kept them well-sealed in oil these many years. In such a dry climate, they showed no age. They were in almost perfect condition.

Jubal was tired. This day, at the end of the week, was usually a time of peace. For a bit of relaxation, he worked the rescued beams. Careful oiling prevented cracking and splintering. He tried to concentrate on the work, sensing the beauty of the grain. Jubal's hands moved slowly and methodically. Jubal's mind wandered to the fellow he had seen around the town. This had been a mystery these last few days.

Jubal knew about him without asking. This man was a carpenter. The scars on the hands of the Galilean were those of a carpenter. The crude tools used even in the best shops often slipped and gashed. Their scars betrayed the career of the man. This fellow, Jesus, seemed very common in some ways. Some in town said he was rightly the king of the Jews.

How could a carpenter be the king of the Jews? Well, Jubal thought that might not be a bad idea. After all, Jubal, himself, might have made a superb king. Did Jubal not have the answers to the problems the nation was facing? He grinned mischievously at the thought. Did Jubal not have as much intelligence and faith as the priests and governor?

Maybe it was only right to name a carpenter as king of the Jews. It was not such a bad idea after all!

This man was so plain, so simple, so common. Perhaps he could not control the nation. He was no threat to the Romans. Even the Jews who sold out to the Romans were not afraid. Maybe he was not a good carpenter, either. Control is always important to a carpenter. Using the tools and shaping the wood called for an exquisite touch.

Jubal found something a too kind about this man, too good to die bound to the gateposts of redemption. Jubal saw something too compassionate and lovable about this condemned man. Where was the cry for justice, and power, and patriotism? A strong king always possessed these. Where were the commanding physique and powerful voice? This fellow before Jubal seemed a little soft-spoken, even tender.

Just a few weeks ago, Jubal had worked to widen the

temple gate. It had to be ready for the chariot of the messiah. Working at the gate, he could bring the old gatepost timbers back to the shop.

Jubal ran his hands along the new construction at the temple. As he finished, his mind wandered far off. This stranger had come to stand beside him. It seemed they shared a vision. They talked a little about the rebuilding. Jubal talked about getting the posts. He told Jesus what he hoped to do with them. Jesus had seemed genuinely interested as perhaps only a carpenter might be. He said he expected to see the timbers in some very significant project very soon. They laughed together.

Now, days later, on the day after Passover, Jubal worked quietly, alone in his shop. Thousands of noisy pilgrims filled the temple rooms and spaces. Jubal stayed with his work. In the little shop in the temple complex, quiet reigned. While Jubal worked and thought, a guard came from the prison. "We need another cross right away. We have three men to nail up today. Some of Barabbas' rioters tore up and burned some of our crosses. We need another one, quickly!"

Jubal had made some crosses before, so this was not a new request. "Who's the cross for?"

"It's for Barabbas. That's why they tore up the others. That's also why we need this cross quick. The captain says to get him strung up before they can do any more damage."

Jubal did not usually think about whether what he was doing was right. He just followed orders. He had little interest in politics.

This Barabbas, Jubal had heard about him. Jubal hated to see his good timbers used for such a thing as killing someone. However, now it was all the suitable timber available. Besides, this man Barabbas deserved to die, Jubal thought it was fitting.

So Jubal and the guard quickly laid out the timbers. Jubal notched the longer one slightly with a heavy axe. Then he tied the shorter post into the notch with a length of leather cord. Jubal disliked driving extra nails into the wood to hold the cross together. These nails always left permanent scars. He knew these pieces would be back in the shop when their work was done. He must try to protect them from more damage.

The cross was always a simple piece of work. Even in this, Jubal took some pride in his speed and his skill. In a few moments the cross was ready.

The guard, a big strong fellow, struggled briefly with the cross. He then headed out the door and up through the palace to the portico. The trial was just finishing. Another guard whipped Jesus as the cross arrived. The crossed acacia planks arrived just in time to go with the parade to Golgotha. Other guards took the cross and laid it across

Jesus' shoulder.

It was about time for Jubal to take a morning break. Jubal went out the back door of the little shop. He walked around to the front of the palace so he could see the excitement. He had never seen Barabbas and was curious about him. How could anybody be so cruel as this man?

Jubal also wanted to see what happened to his good timbers. Jubal climbed onto a stone wall. From there he could watch the excitement.

Jubal could see a man's back. Blood flowed scarlet from the marks and stripes of the whips. He struggled to carry the cross along.

The guards and the mob tried to lay the cross on the condemned man. Jesus fell to the pavement, exhausted and beaten. They kicked and whipped Jesus to make him stand with the cross. He could not.

Now the mob was in control. The soldiers had lost all control as the mob turned to a frenzy of death. The mob shoved the cross onto the back of a black man standing close.

Typical, thought Jubal. Typical.

Then Jubal realized the man on the ground was someone familiar. His eyes rested on someone he met earlier.

Who could this man be, this man whom they knew to be so terrible? He was even a hated man, a known criminal. Even the court and the crowd had substituted him for the violent Barabbas. He was clearly a danger to everyone.

Who was the substitute? Who was this unfortunate soul? Who is so evil even the followers of Barabbas turn their backs on him? Surely he will rot in Hades for what he has done. Whatever it was.

The mob picked the man up. Jubal watched, stunned, maybe even terrified, to see those eyes. They were the eyes of another carpenter, this fellow Jesus. They opened slowly. Jesus' half-blinded eyes seemed to pierce deep into Jubal's soul.

Then he was gone.

# 62. Into Your Hands
John 19:38-42; Isaiah 52:13-53:12;
Psalm 22; Hebrews 10:16-25
The death of Jesus.
Saturday before Easter    Gospel Time: 550

The little procession neared the gateposts of the temple. Bystanders along the walk began to join the moving group. This was a really high moment for everyone in the execution of any condemned man. At the gate, the prisoner had the right to move over to the gateposts. He could touch both posts as a symbol of his loyalty and faith. He could even hold the gateposts close for a few seconds.

The prisoner now held the posts to his bleeding chest. The guards, the judge, the onlookers gathered around all knew he had his own sacred moment. It was his final opportunity to set himself right with the Lord. Even now he could consider himself to have spoken of faith with and loyalty to the temple. He could go to his death at peace with the high priest and the nation of Israel. In the hearts and minds of everyone involved, they could say nothing more. Then he was forced to stumble on to the whipping post.

Jubal served the temple many years as its chief

carpenter. He replaced these gate posts only a few months ago. The old posts were worn smooth from the hands and arms of faithful Jews. Pilgrims and condemned men and women alike left their marks on the posts. Now, after centuries of standing as pillars of faith, the gate required new posts. All this was part of Herod's work of rebuilding the temple. The crews worked to replace or repair the gates, the walls and the roofs. The temple walls were sandstone blocks the size of horses or chariots.

Jesus willfully lost himself for a moment as he surveyed the construction through tear-blinded eyes. He sensed both the strength of the stones and the prideful futility of the construction. Then without a word the group moved on to the whipping post.

12. . . . 13. . . . 14 . . . Jesus lost track. Whipping took its toll on his senses. After fifteen or sixteen blows, the pain changed. Each blow no longer left a mark on Jesus' awareness. His senses became only foggy realities in the chaos. Jesus no longer counted the blows on his back and sides. He felt only the overwhelming steady pain.

For the condemned prisoner and the temple hierarchy alike, the blows finally had to stop. The pain that numbs more pain brings a terrible relief. Any whip blows beyond this did not really cause more agony. The added lashes could only take away any sensitivity to the coming pain. Nails in the hands and feet should bring terrible pain. For

Jesus an so many others, they did not. Even the pain of a spear in the torso could cause no more pain. This point brought relief to the priests and temple guards.

The sentence for Jesus was twenty lashes from a soldier's whip. Some criminals received more, some less. Sometimes the soldier claimed to lose count. He often added a few more swings. He just needed to be sure he had given at least twenty. Sometimes he stopped the whipping one blow short of the sentence. He could not overshoot the count without penalty. For most condemned prisoners, only about the first ten blows or so mattered anyway. After that, every moment of life was a mass of pain.

The soldier who whipped Jesus, Joses from Philippi, was an expert. He knew how to swing the leather rope to cause exquisite pain. He swung his arm and body to wrap the long whip around Jesus' torso. Maximum pain came with this blow. The small metal pieces embedded in the end of the whip dug into Jesus' chest.

The whip left trails of torn skin on his back. A rain of lashes began to break down the body for death. Blood trickled down his back and sides as Joses continued. 17 . . . 18 . . . 19. . . . Joses quietly rolled up the whip as the others let Jesus drop from the post. His beaten body fell limply to the ground. Jesus was nearly unconscious now with pain and terror.

The soldiers knew their duty. The task of the moment was to kill this man. Fulfilling their duty would the spectacle of his death a show of the greatest possible suffering . Taking the life was not difficult, for this criminal did not protest. These men were not a parade unit. Soldiers attached to the local Roman power often battled freedom fighters around and in Jerusalem. All these soldiers were prepared to defend themselves from local patriots. Crucifying this man, named a traitor by temple bosses, was just part of their job. It was part of stopping those who disobeyed the law of the land.

So the soldiers cared little about Jesus. They only knew they had to get Jesus and the cross to Golgotha right now. This day was moving on toward night. Sabbath eve was the only night free of freedom fighter attacks. The king's commander probably ordered an attack on some guerilla hangout tonight. An afternoon of rest in the shade of some tree would help a lot. Even the preparation for the coming battle tonight held terrible tension. The men knew they could die at any moment tonight.

Tomorrow comes the sabbath. According to Jewish tradition, the body must be in the ground before sundown tonight. No devout Jew, especially a Zealot, could touch a corpse on the sabbath. If he did, a long process of ritual cleansing must begin. No one, Jew or Roman, wanted to be part of these ritual prayers and chants.

Springtime Jerusalem days are hot. In addition, the heat of the day helped death come sooner. The sun and loss of water took care of the rest. They just had to get this man onto the cross so he could die quickly.

The soldiers began to pick up Jesus and the cross. One of them spotted a Black man among the spectators. Simon was a silver trader from Cyrene, a small city of northeastern Libya. His dark skin made him stand out from the crowd along the road to Golgotha.

Instantly someone pulled Simon from the shadows. The soldiers laid the 80-pound cross on his shoulders. They prodded him up the street alongside Jesus. Jesus and the procession moved slowly but steadily. Neither the soldiers nor the guards were in any hurry to finish the job. They just knew it must be done so Jesus could die quickly. He must be in the tomb before dark.

Simon slowly led the parade out through the gate of the city. Some remembered Jesus' entry into the city earlier. On that day, many cut branches from palms and waved them at the parade. They shouted "Hosanna! Prepare the way of the Lord!" On this day, a few boys cut more fronds and waved them. The same ones again cried "Hosanna! Prepare the way of the Lord!"

Simon pulled the cross up the short path to the top of Golgotha. Already, two other condemned men hung on Roman crosses on the hill. A third crucifixion in one day was very unusual. The expected crucifixion of Barabbas created a special need. Some of his followers broke into the storage area. They used axes and rocks to break up one crosses. If Barabbas were to die, it would not be with this cross.

The third execution in one day was very rare. Two crosses in use plus an extra should have been enough. This third crucifixion was rare. The temple guards had to find wood from the temple carpentry shop immediately. If they could not find wood quickly, Jesus' must wait two more days to die.

The cross the guards provided was just two heavy pieces of hard black acacia. Several centuries as doorposts at the temple gate made them nearly as hard as iron. Long leather straps laced the pieces together. The arm of the cross hung behind the upright. This practice pulled the prisoner's arms back into a shallow "V". Roman soldiers used the position to force more light and heat from the sun.

The guards nailed the condemned to the cross with their face to the south. If the person pulled or twisted too much, they could easily dislocate their own shoulders. A dying prisoner might hang there in the hot desert sun for days before death.

Sometimes the Romans used a single pole for a death machine. They simply raised the condemned prisoner's arms over his head. Nails held the arms and feet to the pole as it dropped into the ground.

The cross was more dramatic. One could hear the dying wail of the prisoner a long distance away. Tradition held that the sound could be heard even into the Holy of Holies within the great temple. This did not matter to the guards. After all, the real purpose of the cross was entertainment of the powerful. Things have not changed.

Crucifixion nails were very sharp. The guards used the nails repeatedly. A soldier cleaned blood and bits of flesh from them after every execution. He honed them carefully on the hard sandstone of Golgotha. The nails must be sharp. The soldiers simply pushed them through Jesus' hands and feet. Then the nails had to be sturdy. The soldiers drove them into cracks in the acacia posts.

The soldiers stretched Jesus onto the cross. They laid his hands over cracks in the wood. This was the only way they could hold his hands. They drove the nails through his hands, then into the cracks in the wood. Otherwise, the wood was just too hard. Sometimes the soldiers tied the prisoners to the wood with leather straps. Some soldiers had a misguided notion this was a less cruel method of bringing death.

However, this only stretched out the hours until the end came to the prisoner. Is it best to die quickly from a sword or spear? Is it better to hang on the cross from nails in hands and feet? The position dislocated shoulders. The dislocation will tear the abdomen open. Whip cuts will cover the back. Cruel spectators will laugh at the sight.

The soldiers stood the cross and Jesus in a crack in the rock. As they raised it, the base slipped down into the handy crevice. Many fist-sized rocks lay around on the ground. These rocks served occasionally when the sentence was stoning rather than crucifixion. The soldiers packed some of these rocks into the crevice. This kept the cross from falling over as Jesus struggled against his death.

Stoning was quicker than crucifixion, but not nearly so dramatic. It also left blood on the hands of many people. Paid soldiers handled the crucifixion. Stoning, by tradition, was a job for the accusers and witnesses. In Jesus' case, the temple priests, even the high priest, usually threw the first stones. The sentence of crucifixion relieved the temple personnel of this duty.

The Roman army group commander ordered Amosa, a soldier from Lebanon, to hasten Jesus' death. Amosa really did not relish his work, but he had killed men at other times. He also knew he must please the Romans and the temple people as well.

Now he simply drove the sharp iron point of his spear into Jesus' side. The spear cut into Jesus' bladder, intestine, stomach and kidney. Body fluid ran out of

Jesus' side as Amosa pulled the spear away.

Amosa was very careful to not pierce Jesus' heart. Sometimes a soldier missed, and jammed the blade into the heart. This brought instant death for the criminal, but it counted as an error. It denied the crowd their entertainment. Even the temple priests were disappointed with this. The cruel mob needed the pleasure of watching Jesus die. They expected him to struggle for hours, writhing in death on the black acacia posts. Amosa was in deep trouble if he denied the crowd their simple pleasure.

Yesterday, soldiers nailed the other men to their crosses on Golgotha. Neither had to endure the whipping. Both were in much less pain than Jesus. They would live longer, but with less pain. They were thieves who were no threat to the temple hierarchy. Their death or life meant little to anyone but the Lord.

The soldiers whipped or beat Jesus occasionally. Pilate somehow thought this might satisfy the temple people. This cruelty might even save Jesus from crucifixion. This thought was hopeless. The slow, methodical pace seemed to work the crowd to a lather of virulent abuse. They wanted Jesus to die.

Only the cruel jokes and taunts of the crowd broke through this barrier to pain. Temple shills hung around Golgotha through the first few hours of the crucifixion. They yelled out cruel jokes and crude prophecies at the men on the crosses. In the afternoon Jesus lost more of his grip on life. His head dropped lower and lower. Nothing hurt beyond this threshold of maximum pain sensitivity. This loss of feeling was the first step of death for Jesus. He knew he was trying to fight against the loss of pain. The terrifying relief from pain pointed the way. The final release from pain was only a matter of time.

Jesus saw a disciple whom he loved. There, standing next to Jesus' mother. "Momma, he is your only son now."

Then Jesus looked at the disciple beside Mary. "Brother, take care of your mother. I can not." Then Jesus seemed to rest a little.

Jesus hung on to life as the day wore on. His body lost much digestive juices and blood to the sun and Amosa's spear. Some fluids escaped his internal organs and flowed around his heart and lungs. All this loss of blood and water slowly brought his brain to a complete shutdown.

In the heat of the afternoon, Jesus cried out "I am thirsty!" A spectator brought him the traditional and legal drink of hyssop. While it was only a mild narcotic, every drop was welcome. The priests thought this was funny. The soldiers did not care, so they allowed Jesus to sip it. He would die soon, anyway.

The narcotic began taking over his dying system. Jesus hung lower and lower on the cross as the day moved along. His shoulders appeared to pull backward, away from his body. Flies buzzed around him, then lit on his face to lap his sweat. Jesus lifted his face to the heat of the sky.

Then Jesus gasped for breath. Slowly he lifted his head and opened his mouth to speak. His voice was not more than a whisper. The sound rolled around Golgotha and all the hills of the holiest of all lands. It echoed like the sound of near thunder. "Father, into your hands I place my spirit!"

His body and his whole world came apart as he neared death. It seemed the whole earth was silent for at time. No birds sang. No more flies buzzed around him. Lizards refused to scamper around the rock. Even the last handful of spectators now sat or stood silently. Many felt only boredom at the death of a good man.

Now in the silence Jesus cried out into the growing shadows with a voice heard until today. As he spoke, it seemed the whole earth paused. It drew its breath sharply, preparing for the last moments of Jesus. "It is finished!"

Instantly a tremor shook Golgotha and all of Jerusalem. The new walls of the temple, rebuilt by Herod the Great shook violently. Cut stones the size of chariots rattled against one another. The great drape of the holy of holies tore loose from its hooks. The caretakers cried in fear as it fell to the floor.

Without a word, the disciples and women took Jesus' body to the tomb of Joseph. This faithful man offered his own tomb for burial. They buried him in a borrowed tomb. Even in death, he had no nest of his own.

Then they returned to wait for the close of the sabbath.

# 63. The Tomb
Luke 24:1-12; Matthew 28; Mark 16; John 20
Psalm 118:1-24; Isaiah 65:17-25;
1 Corinthians 15:19-26; Acts 10:34-43
Death cannot hold Jesus.
Easter Sunday    Gospel Time: 560

The soft awareness of her presence in his life. Her gentle touch. He somehow felt her arms holding his lifeless body close to her own warmth. The others wrapped him carefully in the burial cloths. Something about her love crept into his senses as he lay still and cold.

He could not yet see her with his eyes. He could only see with his semi-consciousness the woman he loved so deeply. Her eyes looked straight down at him, even without light.

In the dark, his passions drifted across the years. In and out of his feelings ran painless sensations of touch and smell and hope. Sometimes his awareness seemed to come close to the surface of his being. Sometimes his senses hid from him like bats escaping the sunlight, returning to the cave. In and out of reality. In and out of life. In and out of his mother's arms ran the sensations. He did not know where they went or how they returned.

He only knew she was part of his quiet existence.

She sat still now on the garden rock. Bitter tears once flowed down her sun-darkened cheeks. Now the tears for her son were dry. A day and a half of mourning and sobbing robbed them of needed liquid. Mary sobbed, but without tears, now.

Perhaps it was Mary's fault. She could only wonder if her talks with him caused his pain in any way. When she told him about the visits from the angels, he laughed. He seemed caught up in the possibilities of being the messiah. His eyes brightened and his skin grew warm as she spoke to him. The promises of the Hebrews seemed to catch and hold his life and mission.

Now Mary could only wonder. She must have been dreaming, all along. Jesus was gone now. Gone forever. The carpenter's son, dead. No more vision of the messiah. No hope as the son of Man.

Yet Mary could still love. She knew her love for her son lived on in her heart. Now she felt love for her son reaching out across the valley of death. Strangely, that love, reaching out, seemed to strengthen her. She was stronger now, reaching out in love, than in doing nothing.

Perhaps it was the power of her love that moved Jesus. No matter. Jesus faintly sensed her love. For the moment, that was enough. It was good. His mind barely sensed the goodness, but it was enough.

The stone bench of the tomb was cold. Even wrapped in the temporary burial cloths, he was still cold. Only his mother's loving presence in his senses gave him warmth in the dark. He lay quietly on the rock. No breath entered his lungs in the dark of the tomb.

Mary knew daylight was coming soon. Then, for the last time, she prepared herself to enter the tomb. Mary of Magdala, and the other Mary and Martha would be along soon. She needed them around her for what had to be done. The little group would carry some good oil for Jesus' wounds. They brought spices to rub on Jesus' cold body. Their little care was all they could do now.

For the last time, Mary would caress his body with her tender hands. In so many ways, this had been her time with him. Soon after Jesus was born, Mary cleaned him well. A cloth she once carried from Nazareth to Bethlehem for this purpose served again. Mary cleaned his tiny body then just as now. Then she rubbed his body with olive oil as every mother tries to do.

Back in Nazareth, Jesus grew as any other boy. His body suffered little cuts and scrapes. Mary gently caressed those wounds. With a little oil, she tried to give healing energy to Jesus with her hands. This helped his body heal then. He could sense the love.

Now in the tomb, Mary knew his body needed the oil. She could not heal the stripes from the soldier's ships on his back. The grieving mother could not heal the wounds in his hands from the nails. She could not heal the spear wound in his side. She could not scab the punctured skin on his head. Something – or someone – told her she needed to put oil and spices on his body. She just needed to do that in her love for him.

In her mind's eye, Mary began to rehearse the task that lay ahead of her. The oil and spices were ready. The women had gathered fresh cloths after sundown last evening for wrapping his body. Had she forgotten anything?

As she prepared herself to go, Mary heard and felt the other women coming close. They moved slowly together toward the tomb at first light. Their love for Jesus was not that of his mother. It was somehow different. Their presence helped Mary feel stronger.

Their love for Jesus was strong, and certain, even in death. Whether or not Jesus was the messiah was not important. That was just not an issue now. The women only cared that this man they loved was dead. Killed by the temple priests and the Roman government. Right now, he lay on the cold stone bench of the tomb. He waited for their soft hands on his body.

Jesus lay quietly, sensing the love between himself and his mother. His senses drifted toward others he loved. This was not a one-way love. He knew they loved him as well.

The other women were so warm, and good. The miracle of his mother's touch opened him to new life. It helped him remember and feel the touch of the other women. He sensed Mary Magdalene, the other Mary, and Martha. Jesus briefly sensed the reality of so many others of his life. The smiles. The laughter. The tears. The healing. The hope for new life. His mind cleared a little as he nestled in his memory.

The men were good to him. He felt strong in their presence. Jesus grew up with Thomas. Now Jesus needed the love and strength of an old friend.

Peter, the clown. He was always good for a laugh. Jesus used the name "Peter," or "Rock," once for Simon, and it stuck. Everyone guffawed at the joke, even Simon. The name stuck.

In his mind's awareness, Jesus began to feel the others. James and John, and old Zebedee. All of them were so much a part of his life! It was a good life. No one but Jesus seemed to see the dangers ahead for all of them. Judas was not so close as the others. He seemed to stay a little distance from the group as they walked or talked. He seldom laughed at the jokes. Sometimes the disciples sang or just talked quietly as they walked together. Judas seldom joined in. He often appeared to try to be the controlling figure with the group.

Oh, he was useful, all right. As Jesus lay semiconscious in the tomb, he remembered Judas' work. Judas kept the purse for the little band. Jesus and his band went from town to town, talking, preaching, healing. Converts and faithful pressed support onto them. Sometimes it was a coin or two. More often came food or clothing.

Whenever someone offered coins, Judas took church of holding and spending them. None of the others seemed to understand the use of money. As Jesus lay in the tomb, his image of Judas suggested money. The image was confused and hazy to Jesus' struggling mind.

Again, Jesus' mother's love came into his foggy consciousness. He began to feel again her touch on his face and hands. Now her presence seemed a little stronger. The grace in her purpose and love in her heart gave new power. Mary moved even closer to the still form in the distant tomb.

Jesus wanted to move toward her but could not. His body now lay limply on the stone bench. His drive to move in the direction of his mother overwhelmed him. The tension from the frustration in his heart began to change his heart. He knew Mary was coming to him.

As she drew closer, Jesus' heart grew tense. Each of Mary's steps along the path to the tomb changed him. Mary was still so far away from her son! She could not yet see the tomb. The mother's love for her son spanned the distance. It grew stronger as she came closer and closer to his body.

Mary walked very slowly with the other women. The timing of her steps did not change. With each step she sent a powerful wave of love to her son. He only laid in the tomb. Cold. Each wave tensed up his heart in the darkness. After a time, his heart seemed to tense and release, tense and release.

Mary came closer now. Jesus' heart seemed to catch a tide of love from his mother and the others. The energy of that love seemed to let his mind move over these events. The garden at Gethsemane. The trials. The cross. Simon carrying the cross. The nails. The painful crown of thorns. He could now even see the sign above his head.

As Jesus lay on the cold stone bench, he seemed not startled by his situation. These events did not frighten him now, or cause him to marvel. It just seemed he had more to do.

Slowly and carefully, though, Jesus sat up on the side of the stone bench. He pulled the temporary burial cloths away from his face. Some fell around his neck. Some fell to the floor of the cave. Jesus crouched under the low ceiling of the tomb. He saw someone had rolled a large flat rock across the entrance.

At a glance, Jesus knew somehow, some way, he had to move that stone away. It easily weighed much more than he did. Moving that stone would not be easy for a tired, torn and stabbed body.

Jesus moved his crippled body against the round rock. As he strained against the massive stone door, he felt a presence beside him. Jesus no longer pushed alone against the rock.

The top of the rock fell away from the tomb. It landed against another rock and split into two pieces in the darkness. Jesus sat on a piece of the stone, his head in his hands. The cobwebs from his brain seemed to prevent any rational thought.

In the darkness, Jesus heard the quiet voices coming up the path. The moon was nowhere in the sky overhead. Only light from the stars guided the women up the narrow path to the tomb. At first, the women could not see either Jesus or the other figure sitting there.

Jesus' mother could not come close to the entrance of the tomb. Mary's path seemed to narrow and rise steeply on the hill. She suddenly felt tired and discouraged. She could not face going on to the tomb to care for her son.

Mary of Magdala was the first voice Jesus heard. "The rock across the door of the tomb is too big for us to move." Her voice lifted Jesus above his own struggle. Mary always set out to do more than Jesus asked of her. Now, in the earliest morning light, Jesus expected Mary to be first at the tomb.

Joanna answered. "When we laid his body in there, the soldiers helped us. Maybe together we can move the stone a little. Perhaps James and John will come along soon."

The others nodded in silent agreement. With all of them putting all their strength into it, they might move the rock. They might open the gate just a little.

In the darkness, Mary of Magdala saw the stone gate was pushed aside and broken. She began to sob violently. "Someone has taken him. He is gone. Why did they do this? We have to find him!"

Jesus was more alert now. Lifted by the presence of people who loved him, Jesus went on. The man who had completely failed two days ago was ready. The new world order became a reality in the next few seconds.

Jesus quietly stood beside the women as they cried. He smiled a little loving smile now. Then he changed the world as he spoke.

"Are you looking for someone? I am hungry. Did you bring something to eat?"

# 64. Angel
Mark 16:1-13; Matthew 28:1-10;
Luke 24:1-12; John 20:1-10
Easter
Jesus needs a little help.  Gospel Time: 570

This was a terrible work, even when things went easily. His world was almost the worst of all Judaean worlds. They scattered Jews into every part of the known world. They were in Egypt, Nigeria, India, Spain, Ireland, Norway, everywhere. This fate of Moshea was the worst in all the world for a Jew. In his own eyes he ranked even below the Canaanite pig farmers of Phoenicia. Moshea tried to live in the best world he could, but he had no hope of ever doing any better.

Everything he did was wrong. Shortly after his marriage, the village rabbi diagnosed the red splotches on his skin as leprosy. Today we would call it psoriasis. Not then. Leprosy it was.

Moshea tried to keep going. His beautiful wife, Lanor, tried to work with him. She believed they could keep the family together in spite of his leprosy. The two had so much love between them that it should be possible to keep going.

Preserving the family was not easy. Jewish law said

that once they diagnosed a person as a leper, life was basically over. They must not see A leper inside the city, even with family. The leper was to live as an outcast.

Many cities had communities of such social rejects. They lived a little way away from town. Their houses were caves, or simple shacks. Sometimes people brought them food. This offering was usually left at some know place outside the gate by a friend or some family member. Often, the food did not appear. Many lepers simply starved to death in their only home.

Moshea had a different arrangement. The home Moshea and Lanor built together was on the very edge of the community. It had a door facing the center of the community. It also had a door facing the house next door. That door had access to the open field beyond the village. The house next door belonged to his brother, Ashkan.

When the priest diagnosed Moshea with leprosy, this arrangement worked as well as anything could. Moshea had a trade as a metal worker. He spent most of his days mining for metals. Sometimes he smelted or worked his metal in a simple forge in the community of the lepers. He made many items which Lanor could sell in the marketplace or by his brother, Ashkan.

Their arrangement worked well. Each evening, Moshea brought home jewelry, or wire, or even small ingots of metal. Lanor either sold them in the market, or passed them to Ashkan to trade in some other village. In the morning, before daylight, Moshea slipped out of the house to return to the village of lepers.

Some neighbors knew, but no one else was convinced Moshea really had leprosy. It just did not look quite right. His lesions were not black, or running, or with blisters. His rash was bright red. His joints hurt a lot now. Moshea had much difficulty walking long distances. He kept going in the best way he could.

It hurt. His whole life hurt. He had a wife he adored, and who both loved and needed him. His brother was also a faithful friend, but others must see them together. Moshea's legs and feet hurt. His hips hurt so much he could not sleep.

Most of the community assumed Ashkan simply took a second wife, Lanor. Society expected this. They even required it among small village Jews. Most easily adopted the practice here. Moshea and Ashkan built their homes next to each other on the outskirts of town, years ago. Now their foresight was paying off.

Moshea wanted so much to be involved in the synagogue and the temple, but he could not. He wanted to be part of worship, and the discussions of the elders, but they did not allow him in. He was a leper.

The great hurt of Moshea's life lay in what he had become. Because he could no longer walk far, or lift much, he was limited. He could no longer search for sources of copper, gold or silver. The only source he could find was in the caves. That's right, the caves where they laid the dead to dry or decompose. The precious metals were there because family and friend often left simple jewelry on the body when at burial. Then grave robbers like Moshea came within a few days to steal the metal and precious stones.

For the lepers and orphans and other outcasts, it was the only way to stay alive. For Moshea, it was also the source of terrible pain.

Then came the day Ashkan began hearing stories of a new healer from Capernaum. North of the Sea of Galilee, Capernaum and Bethsaida were said to be sacred places. Local folklore said that miracle healings were common. Disabled persons, blind, deaf and many others knew the power of the healing touch. So Ashkan told Lanor, and Lanor told Moshea. She knew Moshea had talked about making a pilgrimage to Bethsaida to try to find healing. However, his bad knees and hips did not allow the four hundred mile journey to Bethsaida and back to Jerusalem. He was just lost.

Now Jesus had come from Capernaum and Bethsaida. The rumors were strong and gave him hope, if they were true. The stories said he made the lame walk in Galilee. Some said Jesus used the miracle powers of the Healing

Pool of Bethsaida. He simply told people to wade in those clear waters from the sacred spring.

Moshea heard so many tales of Jesus. Jesus made the blind see. Jesus healed the epileptic. Jesus healed lepers. Jesus did this, and Jesus did that.

The most important rumor Moshea heard was that Jesus healed lepers! One certified leper cured would have been enough to set his heart on fire. Multiple lepers cured; perhaps ten, or twenty! Even just hearing a brief rumor made Moshea cry a little. Moshea felt a temptation to throw a little pity-party for himself after hearing the news. This certified leper forced himself to keep moving, keep trying to make something good happen.

As the days sent along, Moshea learned from Lanor and Ashkan that Jesus was in Jerusalem. He was healing blind and crippled. They assumed he healed lepers as well, although no one had seen it.

This was almost too much for Moshea. He had to figure out a way to see this Jesus, even at the great risk of it all. He could lose his loving wife, and his brother, and his few friends among the leper community.

Moshea knew the potential cost. A priest diagnosed him. Then the village elders confirmed their witness. It was a terrible risk for him. Even to be seen walking within fifty paces of non-lepers was a death sentence. If they caught Moshea on the street, every citizen was a danger to him. Every person around was perfectly within their rights to join the stoning party immediately. They could and would carry out the death sentence. If someone found him in his own home, they could burn his home. The community would stone his wife and perhaps his brother as well. It all was a horrible fate.

Moshea left his home early that morning. Before the first light of dawn came over the low ridges above Jericho, Moshea was ready to go. He held Lanor just a little longer. "I must see this Jesus, if I can figure out how." The words were heavy in the cold morning air.

Lanor knew their meaning. She knew Moshea might not return that night, or the next, or ever. She knew, also, that Moshea must risk the exposure required. He needed at least some chance of being healed. Lanor knew, and she cried. She kept up her daily routine of cleaning, and helping with the jewelry, but she knew. She prayed.

In the early morning light, Moshea walked into Jerusalem through one of the smaller side gates. Hundreds of people entered the main city every day through these gates. Unless insurgents threatened some sort of invasion, or an armed uprising seemed likely, no one paid attention. Another working man carrying simple metal ornaments through the gate was no concern. He could have been just another craftsman coming to sell his wares in the agora, the marketplace. With his loose robe sheltering his body from the cold, he was well hidden. Even seriously any prying eyes would not know him. Moshe could not have been more anonymous.

Inside the city, Moshea sat down in the marketplace where he could see most of the action. It was a good spot for his needs, although he would not sell much of his jewelry. Very little street traffic passed in front of him. Shade from a high wall shaded his spot so he was not very obvious. He should not show himself out here. He just had to keep his robe and hood on.

Perhaps he could find out where he might see this Jesus. If he listened carefully, he should hear something without revealing himself.

This did not take long. Within only a few minutes, his heart sank. Moshea learned his mission was in vain. Jesus was arrested yesterday, the first day of the Passover, after the Seder, after the feast.

The word on the street was that Herod's people would try and convict Jesus of something. No one was sure what Jesus did to cause the arrest. Also, no one doubted Herod's people would convict him. If they convicted him, no one could guess what would happen. At it's worst, the outcome might be stoning, or flogging.

Moshea now knew he was on a wasted mission. He had no more purpose staying in the market. As the word spread, the potential customers and the other vendors were moving toward the temple and Herod's palaces. They wanted to see and hear whatever they could about Jesus' trial. No one would be here again anytime soon. Everyone had deserted the agora.

Moshea gathered his meager supply of metalworks into his leather bag. He had not sold a thing. This failure was not as much disappointment as was his failure to see Jesus. Now that Herod's people had arrested Jesus, he had no hope. It did not matter whether the high priest or the government had arrested Jesus. The outcome would be the same in either case. Whatever the sentence would be, the government and the temple people would agree somehow. They always did.

Anyway, Moshea would never see Jesus. That also meant that his only hope for healing was lost. Moshea walked now with his head down, just shuffling along. It really did not matter if someone recognized him. Death, even by stoning, would be a less bitter fate than living as a certified leper for another twenty years.

The road out of Jerusalem led past Golgotha, the Place of the Skull. This was the small hill which had been the death place for condemned prisoners for centuries. The government kept this place as a warning to any who walked by on this main road. If you violate the dictates of the king, this is where you end up. If you violate the temple, you violate the king as well. Even if you believe you are trying to purify the temple, you are still in danger. If you shake the temple in any way, this is where you will die.

Even today, already, two men hung on crosses on the hill. They seemed to still be strong, and not close to death. Perhaps later in the day, but not yet. Probably tomorrow. Or the next day.

Immediately, Moshea was ready to pick up his old habits and hopes. The standard burial style, even for condemned prisoners, was coming. When the men died, their families or friends would collect the bodies. The families and friends could take the bodies off the crosses. They would immediately take the bodies to the area of burial caves.

There, the families straightened and cleaned the bodies for burial. They rubbed the spent flesh with oils and spices, wrapped it in strips of cloth. Then, gently, they laid it in a burial cave. If the family had a little money, they usually included some family jewelry or precious cloth in the burial site. It was a way of honoring and remembering. Then they rolled a large stone across the entrance. The family locked it in place using smaller stones and sticks. This kept animals and small children from entering the cave.

Moshea often came to this cave area. His mind was too numb to feel the shame of his actions. The ghoulish practice of grave robbing was too much to contemplate before he gained his certification as a leper. Now, however, and after today's hopes and bitter losses, being ghoulish seemed to not matter at all. He only had to wait until a family buried one body.

Moshea retreated to a crevice in the rock, away from the burial caves. From his hiding place he could see the caves. Then he would know when burial for one body was complete. He would not know if any metal pieces or fancy material was left with the body. He would only know a body was there.

Late in the afternoon, friends and family brought the first body to the caves. Moshea did not know which of the two this was. It really did not matter. A burial is a burial. The small group gathered around the body to do their work. Four or five women and as many men worked quietly and quickly. The day was late, and the body must be in the ground before dark tonight.

Each cave had its own flat stone to roll across the cave opening. Just before dark, the men rolled the stone into place. Then they locked it into place with smaller rocks.

Most of the group left. Some of them, however, seemed to want to stay near the cave. They may have had no place else to go. About six or seven retreated to a small sheltered area several yards from the cave. Moshea saw this sometimes with other groups. He realized this group expected to just sit and talk until late in the evening, perhaps all night.

This meant he could not go into the cave just yet. He had to wait until they left. However, it also meant a stronger chance these folks would leave precious metals or jewels. He had seen it before.

So Moshea waited. He slept some in his hiding place. Occasionally he woke, listening and looking to see the group. They stayed all night.

In the morning, the group left. Moshea could not risk entering the cave now. Recognition as a grave robber and a certified leper would be a certain death sentence. So Moshea just waited quietly through the day.

Part of the little group came, stayed a few minutes, and left again. When darkness came, Moshea was alone again. He waited a little longer, then carefully approached the cave.

What Moshea had to do next did give him chills. What if the body were still alive? What about ghosts? Was there a demon in the cave, just waiting to pounce on some grave robber who came near? He must be already violating the will of the Lord somehow. Otherwise, why would the Lord inflict on him the punishment of leprosy? Somehow, it just did not matter any more.

Moshea was willing to risk terrible consequences to make a better life for Lanor. He loved her so much he could face any danger now. He had seen the worst which could come to him now.

The area of the caves was quiet tonight. Too quiet. As he neared the cave, he looked around as best he could in the dim starlight. Nothing seemed to be out of place. Except Moshea.

Moshea pushed the boulder against the cave opening just a little. Now he kicked away the small rocks which held the boulder in place. He had opened other caves before, but not this one. The boulder seemed lodged in place, impossible to move.

He put his shoulder to the heavy stone. Carefully, Moshea began to rock the boulder sideways, just a little at first. Right, left, right, left. It seemed the stone moved a little easier with each push. Right, left, right, left. A little bit each time.

Moshea stopped pushing and shoving for a moment to catch a breath. His work was moving the flat boulder just a little.

As Moshea rested, his heart suddenly began to pound against his neck. A hand slowly began to appear through the slim crack Moshea opened between the boulder and the cave opening. "Help me! Help me!"

Moshea wanted to run. This was one of his terrible fears. Was this man alive? Was this a demon? Moshea's own desperate search for support in his struggles locked him into his response. He could not turn away.

Now Moshea's body felt the powerful strength of righteous adrenalin. Another man was hurting. Moshea might be able to do something about it. Throwing his body against the boulder, the leper slowly opened the space around the cave opening.

A big shove from Moshea and help from whoever was in the cave solved the problem. The flat stone fell away from the cave. It broke in half as it fell against another rock in front of the cave. As it broke, the hand came through, then the arm and the shoulder.

Moshea kept working to clear away the rocks around the entry. Finally, the entire man squeezed out of the cave. Moshea could not speak. Exhausted, he could only sit on a half of the broken gate rock.

The man coming out of the cave wore loose burial clothes. Moshea knew that, because the burial came late on a sabbath eve, burial had to come quickly. Preparation was hasty. The mourners would return on the day after the sabbath to finish the job properly.

Who was this man? He was not one of the two prisoners Moshea saw today, still hanging on Golgotha. He was a stranger. That Moshea risked his life to save this stranger did not really matter. They were both alive. Only that mattered.

Moshea did not know how long he sat on the rock with

the strange man. He only knew they were both alive. Finally Moshea heard the women coming up the trail to the cave. One woman sang a hymn softly as she walked. Then she began to ask, speaking to no one in particular, "Who can help us move the rock away?"

It was almost a prayer she spoke. "Will an angel come to help us move the rock? Please, Lord, please send an angel!"

Moshea began to rub his tired muscles and joints as Mary spoke. Mary cried out because she saw the open entrance to the burial cave. Moshea felt again the rough and cracking skin around his hips, knees and shoulders. Now the skin was soft as gentle lambskin.

Somehow Moshea could answer Mary now. He could say the truth. "Do not worry. Do not be afraid. Everything is all right." The truth sounded through the early light. Amen.

# 65. Joseph of Arimathea
## John 19:38-20:23
During the week after Easter.
Gospel Time: 575

Joseph could not believe his good fortune. Although he wore a perpetual smile now, none of his friends or family realized just how much the Lord seemed to be smiling on him. Everything in his life, from his business to his family to his temple life, was coming together in a great rush of comfort and satisfaction.

Joseph always provided a good life for himself and his family. As did many people of that time, Joseph made his living traveling the roads of three continents buying and selling everything he could. Jewelry, medicines, cloth, even his caravan camels and horses.

After years of hard work and sharp trading, Joseph worked himself into a remarkable position. He was able to settle down into the Jerusalem suburb of Arimathea. Southeast of Jerusalem a couple miles toward Hyrcanum, Arimathea offered a wonderful life to its residents. Clean water from a good well, security in the form of Roman forces garrisoned there, and a neighborhood of relatively wealthy commerce-oriented families.

Joseph really was an educated man. He gained most of

his education from the cities and villages where he traded his goods across Europe, Asia and Africa, from Morocco and Britain to India. With about ten men and their women, his caravan made a good picture of moderate success across the Roman roads of the time.

Joseph had some special trading patterns as he moved around the area. One day, early in his career as a traveling merchant, someone approached him to deliver a letter to a relative living in another city. Joseph had told a local person of his plans to visit the second city. Now the word had drifted around town of this plan. Soon, and for a small fee, of course, Joseph placed a beautiful little scroll in a camel pack.

The scroll, written in koine Greek, included several names and addresses in the Aegean seaport town of Thessalonika, near the border of Macedonia. In a few months, Joseph delivered the message, intact and clean, to one of the addressees shown on the scroll. Again, he was given a nice bit of money and a hero's reward of a good feast for his efforts.

Now, Joseph, being a rather sharp trader, recognized a good thing when he saw it. He told several people of his next directions of travel, and more messages showed up to be delivered. This could be a good business, very profitable. In the process, Joseph was able to learn about local customs and literature and religions in the best way possible, from local leaders. He also gathered names of persons who might make good contacts in cities along his route of travel.

Shortly, however, Joseph was able to add yet another level to his commercial life. A common practice of the time was for government workers and artists and commercial traders to join a traveling caravan headed toward a distant locale. This meant security and traveling companionship. For instance, a person traveling from Thessalonika to Athens might join one caravan to Bilota, and another from Bilota to Athens.

Joseph welcomed these travelers into his caravan for many reasons. The money was good, and adding another strong man or two to the troop was always good for security. The roads were long and tiresome, so someone different to talk with along the way was a choice gift. Joseph could hear about new ideas, new governments, and new religions as he traveled. He also learned to speak several different languages. This made trading in different territories much easier.

But after twenty years of this life, Joseph was ready to settle down. He bought two pieces of ground. Then he proclaimed he would never travel again from his adopted village of Arimathea. He could spend his time with his wife, and his children. He could be a faithful worker in the synagogue. He could take a position as a member of the local group of elders.  In short, he was home.

On the first piece of ground, in the heart of Arimathea, Joseph had a home built for himself and his family. Spacious, secure, and comfortable.  Joseph was known widely across the world. Many of his friends and former customers came often to visit him in his new home.  They might stay a few hours, or a few days.  These long time friends were welcome reminders of the travels and conversations of years past.  The talks were still of ideas, philosophies, governments and religions.

The second piece of ground purchased along with the first was a burial cave on a cliff just to the northeast of Jerusalem.  This was the traditional burial grounds for the wealthier residents.  The burial caves were small, just holes large enough to slide in a body or two wrapped in cloths, seasoned with myrrh and crushed aloes.  A large flat stone was usually included in the deal.  It could be rolled across the mouth of the cave and sealed with clay mud to keep out animals.

These two plots of ground, the home and the cave, were important to Joseph for another reason.  First, they were to be his homes for the remainder of time itself, as long as eternity should last.  Everyone understood the symbolism of purchasing the two together.

But second, they were positioned very near the temple of the creator, Yahweh.  Inside himself, Joseph had a third commitment which he intended to keep. On one of his last trading adventures, Joseph brought his caravan south from Damascus. He pushed it through Capernaum, then Bethsaida. Finally he moved it along the eastern shores of Lake Tiberias, the Sea of Galilee.

In Capernaum and Bethsaida, his customers and business contacts constantly talked of a healer and medical worker. This man, Jesus, lived and worked in Capernaum a few years. He did carpentry work and healing around Chorazin, Capernaum and Bethsaida. His fame was as wide in Damascus and Jerusalem as in Capernaum itself.

At first as a side note, he spoke as a prophet and healed many people. His talks began as a call for personal faith, righteousness and healing. After a few months of this, it seemed the Sons and Daughters of Korah got to him. These rebels of the hill country seemed to convince him of the need to call for temple righteousness in the name of Yahweh. His healing work grew, especially in Bethsaida. His call for temple righteousness seemed to become stronger and louder in Jerusalem each month.

Then came a time Jesus gathered more people around himself and announced his mission to Jerusalem. He would go to the holy city and deliver righteousness in the name of the Lord to the temple itself. In a couple days, Jesus and his people were ready to leave.

This was an interesting event. Jesus had close to a hundred people who seemed to be ready for the trip to Jerusalem. However, when Jesus himself left Capernaum, only a dozen or so left with him. But later in the day, the crowd at the tax collector's tent was much smaller than usual. Those remaining agreed that many had left earlier to travel along the western shore of the lake. Others left earlier or later than Jesus, traveling along the eastern shore. Some even began the trek by boat. This seemed to be more of a migration than a pilgrimage to the temple.

When Joseph and his caravan came into Capernaum to trade and rest, he joined the familiar tent flap group. He told the men there of his plans to move down the eastern shore of the lake. They laughingly told Joseph about Jesus. They said he had left a few days earlier on his trek to Jerusalem. They would be traveling slowly, nearly all on foot, and stopping frequently to talk and heal. Joseph would surely overtake them in a day or two.

Joseph of Arimathea stayed in Capernaum a week or so. When the market dried out, he moved on to Bethsaida. Again, the crowds talked mostly about the healer, Jesus. After a week in Bethsaida, Joseph of Arimathea moved his caravan on toward Jerusalem, down the eastern shore of Lake Tiberias. In every village along the way, people told more stories of the healer and prophet. At each stop,

Joseph seemed to be just a little closer to Jesus and his band of disciples.

Finally, at the little town of Gilgal, just outside Jericho, Joseph the trader met Jesus the healer and prophet. Jesus arrived at the camping area just outside the town about two hours before Joseph's caravan. By the time Joseph arrived to set up camp for his caravan, it was late in the day. Jesus' disciples were preparing their meal and gathering the local residents for a talk and some healing.

Joseph asked his people to set their camp close by that of the Galileans. He had two very good reasons for this action. First, he knew enough about Jesus to suspect that Jesus would draw a crowd. They would come for both his talk and his healing. Life in Gilgal was not exciting. In fact, the presence of Jesus and of Joseph's trading caravan at the same time was a hot ticket. Indeed, this might be the most exciting event in Gilgal this year.

Joseph's second reason for parking here was to meet this Jesus now. Joseph heard wonderful tales of Jesus' healing power and his remarkable bravery. People from Gilgal to Capernaum talked about Jesus' harsh prophecies. These blasts were directed at Herod, Pilate and the temple social system. Now Joseph, the trader, had an opportunity to meet the man, face to face.

So for the next two or three days, Joseph talked with Jesus at every opportunity. Sometimes just the two of them; sometimes in a larger group. Joseph found many times to pick Jesus' brain. He tried to understand Jesus in the light of so many others he knew from years past. Jesus talked about healing, and about the temple. He talked about righteousness, and equal justice. He talked, and talked and talked with Joseph.

While Jesus talked, Joseph's caravan helpers traded, bought and sold his goods. When the market in Gilgal dried up, Joseph and the caravan moved on. Jesus would stay in Gilgal another day or two, then go on to Jericho. By the time Jesus reached Jericho, Joseph would be gone on to Jerusalem, or even to Arimathea.

Joseph wanted to get to Arimathea as soon as he could, now. He had purchased the land a year or two earlier for his home and for his family burial site. He arranged for a home to be built on his land in Arimathea. The other site was the site of his burial cave. This next event would be a rather short trading trip, to Damascus, Antioch, Heraclea and return. He left his wife and son home to oversee building the home and digging the cave. Now he wanted to get back to them as quickly as possible.

When Joseph returned to Arimathea, he was in for a real surprise. His family was, of course, very happy to see him. The home they built for Joseph and his family was a wonderful home, spacious and comfortable. He brought them gifts from the north, from Russian and

Scandinavian traders.

But the excitement really came boiling over when Joseph mentioned he spent several hours picking Jesus' brain in Gilgal. He also mentioned he invited Jesus to visit Arimathea during his pilgrimage to Jerusalem. At this point the little crowd erupted with anticipation at the announcement.

So it was that Jesus visited Arimathea several times during his months in Jerusalem. The people of Arimathea seemed to respect Jesus in a special way. They supported his healing work by sending people to him. They were eager to be part of the purification of the temple. Whenever Jesus talked about the temple, the people were fascinated with his ideas.

The people of Arimathea were not as strongly anti-Herodian as were the Sons and Daughters of Korah in Galilee. They did not like Herod, but they could live with him. But they liked this Jesus more and more each time they saw him.

But each time Jesus came to Arimathea, Joseph became a little more concerned for Jesus. Caiaphas, the high priest, was a kinsman of Herod. His wealth grew as the work of rebuilding the temple of Solomon neared completion. As the high priest, he distributed special privileges to his priests and leading laymen in return, of course, for small money gifts.

Jesus now stayed longer in Jerusalem around the temple. His words grew more hostile toward Caiaphas and Herod as time went along.  Finally, a runner came to Arimathea from downtown Jerusalem.  He told Joseph the devastating news.  Caiaphas had arrested Jesus and put him in prison. The trial would obviously be tomorrow.

In the morning, Joseph the known, respected community man, with business contacts all over the Roman world, now worried about his new friend. He went into Jerusalem to learn what he could about Jesus' fate.  Just as he reached the temple, the soldiers were taking the cross from Jesus back.  They laid in on the back of Simon, from Cyrene.  Joseph knew Simon some. They had dealt with each other in two or three towns along the Mediterranean, from Egypt to Morocco.  Simon was a fair man, though a sharp trader.  He just happened to be a black man in town when Jesus was arrested.

Now Simon dragged the heavy cross to the city gate, and out to the Place of the Skull.  The soldiers nailed Jesus to the cross and stood it upright. Then they stood back and waited for him to die.  After some long time, one of the soldiers grew impatient.  Because Jesus did not appear to be dying quickly enough, a soldier violated Jewish tradition and Roman military law.  He used a spear to pierce Jesus' side to bring on death more quickly.

Jesus finally died after a few hours. Joseph went to the

garrison commander of the soldiers, who he know from Arimathea. "Captain, you know how the people of Arimathea feel about this man. I would like to take his body and bury it before sundown. If you keep the body on the cross now, you will have to stay here to guard it through the sabbath. By law, neither you nor us can touch the body on the sabbath."

The commander quickly agreed. The work here was nearly done. The men needed to get back to town. They were already taking the lifeless body of Jesus down from the cross.

Joseph had a couple of his caravan men place Jesus' body on a horse. This horse was a favorite of Joseph. He purchased it from a horse breeder and his daughter in Capernaum. The daughter had some very terrible disease, and could barely walk. Yet she could teach horses to do almost anything. She usually sold the horses to the Roman legions or traveling traders. However, this one was a special sale to Joseph, a family friend.

In a few minutes everything was ready. Joseph sent one of his men into the city to purchase supplies for burial. They would need some plain cloth, and aloes and myrrh. With the rest of his crew, Joseph headed for his newest property, the burial cave.

At the cave, Joseph became aware of others standing around, watching. He recognized Mary, Jesus' mother,

Mary from Magdala, and yet another Mary. There were also three or four men, whom Joseph recognized as having traveled with Jesus from Capernaum.

Joseph had his people bury Jesus carefully. They mixed the myrrh with the aloe pulp and spread the mix over his entire body. Then they wrapped the cloth over his body and tied it around him. Then over his body they wrapped another layer of plain, course cloth to hold the other on him.

The sun was beginning to set by this time, so the men slid the lifeless body into the cave. Just as the last direct rays of light came from the sun, the watching men helped roll the rock across the cave entrance. It was now shielded safely against the weather and animals.

So it was over. With nothing more to do, Joseph and his men, and the disciples left. Only the guard left by the captain remained. His job was to be certain no one disturbed the body. If someone did, it might be possible to then claim some kind of resurrection. He almost succeeded.

Almost.

# 66. Love Talk
Matthew 28:1-10; Mark 16:1-8; Luke 24:13-35
Psalm 114; Isaiah25:6-9; 1 Corinthians 5:6b-8
Two respond to Jesus' new life.
Easter evening, or through week following Easter
Gospel Time: 580

Later that day, that first day of the resurrection of Jesus, life continued. Bartholomew and Kelita walked together through the dusty streets of Jerusalem. The word about Jesus spread fast among the community of faithful. Jesus was no longer in the sandstone. Jesus was alive. He walked and talked.

Even with this news the faithful community could not bear to be together just yet. They could not yet gather to speculate on what might happen to them. For most of the day the community stayed apart. Then, toward evening, they drifted back to their little upstairs room.

Before Jesus' arrest and trial, the disciples spent hours almost every day talking theology with Jesus. Now the confused men tried to know the meaning of Jesus' resurrection. If it were really true, what did it mean? Perhaps even more, they just needed to be together as people who felt Jesus love for themselves. They needed to be together. The little group could draw strength from one another.

As Bartholomew and Kelita walked and talked, they intentionally calmed themselves. The close couple was able now to really share what was on their minds. By their faith, their conversation and the spirit of Jesus in their lives, they changed themselves. The resurrection of Jesus destroyed all their old personal character boxes.

Now Bartholomew and Kelita felt renewed and alive. They did not need to worry about what other people thought about their relationship. The pair was free to worry only about their relationships with Jesus and with each other. Two people in love held hands walking together on the streets of Jerusalem. Holding hands was a strange thing in those days.

Bartholomew and Kelita talked about children and they talked about love. They had the sense of release, complete with forgiveness and grace. Water floods over a spillway when gates are opened. Each new event brings new conversations. Words spill out and find their own channels deep into committed hearts.

For Bartholomew and Kelita, new questions arose about their lives. They spoke afresh about their choice of careers. This small part of Jesus' community talked openly with each other about their sex life. Their feelings about touching each other took new meaning as they began to experience new ways of living.

As they walked along, they thought about the gathering that evening. Nothing was certain in these first few days after the tomb was found empty. They could not know who stayed with the group. They wondered who might pull out. Bartholomew and Kelita knew they had found new ways to love each other. Now they wondered whether this was the way in the whole group.

Kelita's uncle gave them money to purchase supplies for the trip back to Galilee. As they went into the market they felt ready to purchase some special items instead. These articles had nothing to do with the trip home.

Kelita found a cloak, a simple but pretty piece of cloth for Peter. Peter lost his in the scuffle in the garden of Gethsemane when the guards arrested Jesus. In the life of a wandering evangelist, it could be a protection from the wind. It could also become a regal show piece. It could serve as a temporary tent or even a table covering. Nevertheless, Peter would need it as he made the long trek back to Galilee.

For Matthias, the writer and accountant, they found a new pen-quill for record keeping. None of the group was concerned about keeping records for later generations. Matthias only recorded some small pieces of discipleship business. It was the only way Matthias knew to prove his own honesty.

James was the rowdy one who really did not seem to

need anything. He could not have kept it in one piece if he had stored anything away. For him, the prize must be a gag gift, a lemon. The sour lemon might make his lips pucker so he could not talk so much. Bartholomew and Kelita could laugh now at the vision of James with puckered lips.

For Judas, not Judas Iscariot, they found a little carved wooden monkey. This Judas had the name of "Monk" because he was so serious. Everyone liked this Judas. He listened well. He never shared any privacies.

For the others there were a little of this and a little of that. Oh, what a difference a few hours made. Earlier today they were crying, worried about their own lives. Living as escapees from Roman crosses did not attract them. Anyone could catch and murder them. Now they were buying gag gifts for each other out of their joy.

What a difference! Not a total change, for they were still hungry. As all the people of the world, these followers of Jesus still needed to eat.

Bartholomew and Kelita supposed they had all the money found in the little community. The two of them bought several loaves of bread and some wine. The new harvest had just come in. The wine had not had time to ferment and age properly. It just happened to be the cheapest available. They bought it with their precious hoard of coins.

Bartholomew and Kelita left the market feeling good about their treasures. They laughed about the gifts and the changes in their lives. They carried their sack of treasures slowly toward the meeting place outside town. Oh, it was a good day! Their love for Jesus made it that way. They were to be together again. The ability to touch each other with hands and eyes and voice renewed them. Distributing the gifts felt good later in their nostalgia.

As they came to the city gate, an old woman sat huddled in rags. Poor, dirty, homeless, probably very cold at night, she looked pitiful. Bartholomew and Kelita stopped talking as they came near to her. It was as if they really did not have anything to say to each other. They knew each other's thoughts.

First, Peter, the rock, the hard one, did not really need the cloak. He could be warm with some rags until they were all back in Galilee. Besides, in Galilee many young women desired to make a new cloak for Peter. He was eligible, and quite attractive. The cloak spread nicely over the woman.

Down the road under a tree, an aging rabbi sat with a young student. He was teaching the young man the skill of writing and reading. The new writer struggled with a bit of chalk stone on a hard clay tablet. A piece of scroll and worn-out quill lay beside him. Too many hours of pressure from untrained fingers had made it unusable.

Bartholomew and Kelita walked on, smiling. The young man was the amazed owner of a fine new quill. After all, Matthias was too busy for time to do much writing. Besides, the quill would probably be broken before they got back to Galilee anyway.

Now the day was growing hot from the noon time sun. At the first water hole they passed, a family milled about desperately. The small children cried with throats parched from the desert. They could scarcely utter a sound. The parents had counted on finding water here. As water holes will do sometimes, the hole was dry.

Kelita placed the lemon on the ground. Then she kneaded it with her foot to break the juice free. Then she took Bartholomew's knife and cut the lemon in half. She squeezed half into her own water bag. Half she squeezed into Bartholomew's to keep them fresh. Now they had lemon-flavored water for the family, a drink fit for royalty. The children and parents drank their fill. Bartholomew noted they could probably get another lemon for James. James really needed a lemon, sometimes. He really deserved one. Perhaps this one was too ripe and too sweet.

Bartholomew was beginning to notice the sack of gifts. The bag was not as heavy as it had been. Walking was a little easier now.

Down the road a small boy walked slowly along, in tow

behind his mother. Giant tears ran down his face. The tears were such as only a small child can shed. When a chariot runs over a small puppy, it is real tragedy. This was just an accident. The puppy just slipped its leash and ran out into the road. The charioteer stopped and tried to help the puppy, but it was hurt too badly.

It was Bartholomew's turn. Ah, yes, the little monkey making the funny face. Almost every child needs a toy monkey sometime. This was not quite the same as the puppy, but it did seem to help.

One at a time the other gifts tumbled from Bartholomew's sack. Everything went into the hands of strangers. Finally there was left only one loaf of bread and the wine. The bread was a simple loaf, baked early in the morning in a community oven close by. The wine was a few months old, but quickly gaining flavor.

Bartholomew and Kelita talked about this a little. They thought about Jesus who had given and given and given. He gave until he had nothing left to give but his life. The bread and wine seemed to represent Jesus' life in so many ways.

Later in the day when the disciples and the others gathered they talked about Jesus. They wondered aloud about what had happened to them since the empty tomb was found. They began to talk about and name the people they had met in their travels. Then they began to wonder what might have happened to Jesus.

Someone read the words of Moses about the victory of the Lord. As he finished, somehow Jesus was there among them. Somehow, some way, his presence neither surprised nor shocked them. He was among them, talking easily about their common experience and mission. Their own eyes had seen him crucified. The faithful disciples and the women had placed the body in the tomb. Now the group appeared to expect just such a thing from Jesus.

Then Jesus said the strangest thing. "I am hungry. My belly is growling at me. I have not tasted food for three days. Do you have anything to eat? I do not need much. Perhaps a little bread and wine."

The only food was the loaf of bread and the small skin of wine. Bartholomew and Kelita brought them from Jerusalem for the disciples. Sharing them with Jesus was even better. Now Bartholomew laid the bread on the small table. He poured the wine into Elijah's Cup. This beautiful cup stood waiting for the return of the prophet or for the unexpected guest.

Kelita spoke. "Jesus, when we were last together, you took the bread, broke it and blessed it. You passed it out to all of us. Then you said, `This is my body broken for you. Take this and eat it.' Then you passed the cup, Elijah's Cup. You said we should all share. You said `This is my blood poured out for you and for many.' I did not know what you meant when you said these words."

"Now I remember another thing you said one day. You spoke clearly when you gave us your guide. You said when we do something to the least, we do it to you. Perhaps now I understand. Perhaps I can see you and your life more clearly."

# 67. Check It Out, Thomas
John 20:19-31; Psalm 16;
Acts 1:14a-32; 1 Peter 1:3-9
Jesus' boyhood friend makes a leap of faith.
2nd Sunday of Easter, usually in April
Gospel Time: 590

Jesus died on the cross on Golgatha. At that same moment, all hope for the fulfillment of a dream died in Thomas' heart. His entire world lost its truth in those last few hours with Jesus. Every dream Thomas had about a good life suddenly became a nightmare. Every thought about having some benefits from his strong commitment to Jesus and his mission faded away. Any hope to hold his head high before the powerful of the world disappeared. It all died on the cross with Jesus.

Now Thomas had no instinct to go on. He saw no point going back to boats and nets on the sea of Galilee. With no work, no hopes, no emotional bankroll, Thomas saw no life ahead. Fishing for men instead of the products of the lake was not a viable calling any longer. Judas was not the only disciple who might commit suicide.

Thomas hung around with the others in a daze through the sabbath. The small group tried to give each other strength in their prayers. They shared their quiet words and their touches. They gave Thomas special comfort because he had been so close to Jesus. Jesus' own mother tried to give Thomas some comfort, but what was the use? Everything was gone now. Everything. Gone.

On the morning after the sabbath, Thomas was despondent; even bitter. He went again to Golgotha, alone, hoping to find the truth of that place where Jesus died. It plagued him. He tried to shake off the hurt of the Place of the Skull. There he tried to make some sense of all that had happened.

Later, Thomas wandered slowly along the path to the tomb cut in the hill. He sat heavily a few yards from Jesus' grave in the cold sandstone. Thomas told himself to remember the good times the disciples shared with Jesus. He thought about all the wonderful people he met during their travels.

Wherever Jesus and the disciples traveled, crowds seemed to gather as close as possible to Jesus. Many faithful brought food for the group. The crowds seemed to see the offerings of food as tickets to join in the conversation and the healings. Others came just to ask questions. Some seemed to just want to be around the excitement for a time. A little bread or fruit for a few minutes of Jesus' time.

Thomas thought about all those nights around the fire pits of Galilee. Maybe these intimate little gatherings were the best nights of his life. Frank talks, deep questions and honest answers made it all worth while. Laughing over petty squabbles, with horseplay and dark disagreements, also filled the hours. Songs and memories brought intense feelings. Everywhere was Jesus. Even when Jesus was away from the group, he was the center of everything.

Jesus' presence was enough, and it was there always. When the group ate, Jesus filled the very air with his calm self control. When they slept, his strong presence made the night safe. As they walked, they knew Jesus walked beside them. Even when he was away from their path or walking behind or ahead of them, he was beside them.

Sitting beside the tomb, Thomas cried bitterly to himself now. Although he somehow felt the presence of Jesus beside him, he knew better. Jesus was gone for good. Thomas had put everything on Jesus. Jesus had betrayed again his friend again. Jesus was gone, and with it also was Thomas. As Thomas sat silently, it seemed almost as if Jesus sat beside him.

How often they sat together on a hillside such as this, back around Nazareth or Capernaum or Tiberias. How often they talked about life and work and the decisions of the Sanhedrin. It always seemed as if Jesus had a plan of action, something to do next. Thomas was always a part of it somehow, willing or unwilling. Even now it seemed to Thomas Jesus had a plan. Yet . . . of course that could not be. Jesus was dead and gone. He was in that tomb. Right there. Thomas himself helped wrap Jesus and place him in the tomb.

Thomas forced himself to stand up and get moving. He told himself today was the day he, Thomas, the faithful one, must make the break with the others. Most of them, he was sure, were ready to go back to Galilee. The others could return to fishing for a living. Fishing was fine for them. It just did not have any draw for Thomas. He needed to do something else. Thomas was not sure what might work for himself. He could go to the coast, maybe down to Egypt. He would find a place where his fishing skills might be valuable. Anyway, it was "new life time."

Thomas could not know about last evening. All the other remaining disciples gathered in a small room at the inn. Judas, of course, was now dead. The rest were confused and afraid for their lives. They locked and bolted the door, then pulled the shutters on the windows.

Most of the disciples already decided to go back to their old work. Some were ready to fish. Some were ready to build houses, using the materials around Galilee. Some might work for the government, either around Capernaum or north in Damascus. Two or three had even decided to try to stay around Jerusalem. They vowed to remain faithful to restoring the righteousness of Jerusalem. It was still the holiest city of the world. Surely this was something Jesus held in his heart.

After all, Jerusalem was still the holiest city of the world. The holiest place in Jerusalem was still the temple. The holiest spot in the temple was the holy of holies. The beauty of the newly rebuilt temple was almost beyond imagination.

The holiest people of the world were the Jews. The holiest of the Jews were priests, and the holiest priest was the high priest. Once each year the high priest approached the holy of holies. This was the holiest moment in time each year.

Surely Jesus wanted this place to be the most special place on earth. For that to happen, this people must restore this moment and place. It must have the right ethical and spiritual climate. This could be a fine calling for the remaining disciples, even with the death of Jesus.

The disciples and the women came together in that little room for a last meal and to say their farewells. They were ready to get life started again. Several hours later they still sat together, unwilling to part company. They talked, then talked some more.

None of the disciples were really certain how it happened. They simply began to hear Jesus talking to them. He seemed to materialize at the back wall, not near any window. "Take it easy. Everything is all right. You will all be okay."

They heard Jesus say it again. "The Lord's peace is with you. As you live, breathe in the breath of the Lord. It is the will of the Lord you do the work on earth. This includes forgiveness of sin. It includes bringing to reality the kingdom of the Lord on earth."

Jesus left them now again. They were only silent, stunned, confused by the enormity of their task and their call. How could this be?

After another week the disciples met again. They promised to meet the day after the sabbath as often as possible. This time Thomas was with them. He could not miss this occasion for any purpose. Thomas had a little smile in his heart. He had already decided the disciples had too much wine with their dinner last week.

Thomas loved Jesus as much as anyone loved Jesus, but this was a little ridiculous. Jesus had changed Thomas through their relationship. Thomas was no longer the flighty, angry, quick-tempered youth from Galilee. He was no longer willing to get into a fight at the village square.

Now he was more sensible, even practical. Now he could love. Now he could accept love from others. Thomas had matured.

Now Thomas could see ahead. He could even commit himself to fulfilling the work of Jesus. He could wander around doing good. Thomas the orphan could teach everyone to love, and to avoid war. The man who named himself after a violent soldier could teach them to treat each other kindly. Sure, Jesus was dead. His death did not mean Jesus had no more impact on human life. Thomas could never forget him, even if he were dead.

All the others Jesus chose for his group in his thirty years on earth promised to remember their leader. Something about the guy was very special.

Thomas was not ready to fall into the traps that caught the other disciples. They were dreaming dreams, seeing nightmares, experiencing visions. They saw things that could not exist. These otherwise intelligent men and women must be hallucinating. The tension and the turmoil of their lives, and a little wine, must have altered their minds.

The visions did not upset Thomas. They had all been through a lot together. These people were all his friends, good folks. They were just a little hallucinatory, that's all.

Back in the room together, the disciples were ready to break up the old gang. It was time to go their separate ways.

While they remembered the past they told each other of their visions and the new world order. Even with Jesus gone, Thomas still had hopes for that kind of world some day. Even the hope that came through in their words was not excuse enough. They felt in their lives the strength for their continued talk about Jesus. Their hallucinations about Jesus coming back alive almost seemed real.

Thomas finally found himself challenging their words and visions. "Look, friends, I really love all of you. We have been through a lot with Jesus, my brother and your brother. I loved him dearly, just as you did."

"Now, nothing personal in this, but I think you have been hallucinating. I think you found some wine that sat around and spoiled. Now you are seeing things."

"For crying out loud, Jesus is dead. That is all of it. He is gone. He is history now. I saw him die and I helped bury him. I pulled the nails from his hands and feet and carried him to the tomb. Now, until I see hands and feet with nail holes, I do not believe it. Unless I see him walking around, I cannot believe he is alive."

"We carried him to the tomb. I held my hand over the spear hole in his side. I needed to keep him from losing more blood and body fluid. My hand knows exactly the shape of that hole. Unless my hand finds that same hole in a living man, I do not believe. He must be walking, talking, breathing and eating. If not, I will know Jesus is dead. Done. Gone."

"Look. You know how I loved Jesus. You know I did everything I could for him. I am even yet willing to give up my own life. The reality is this. It is over. We must be on about our business. We can still profit from a bad situation. We can live as Jesus said we should. I know what I need to do now."

While Thomas spoke, Jesus came and stood behind him. Thomas was far into his own thoughts. He could not see the faces of the others. He could not see as they looked up at Jesus. Faces of new power, joy, and expectation met Jesus. Some faces showed confusion.

"Hello, Thomas."

Thomas' heart stopped for a moment. His face turned white. He could not even stutter a word or turn his head to look. He knew the voice as well as he knew his own.

"Thomas, do you hear me? Look at my hands. Look close, now, brother. Touch them where the nails were in them. My feet! Be sure to look at my feet. You have washed them for me often. Are they the same feet?"

"After you check my feet, put your hand here. That's it, below my ribs where the guard opened me with the spear. Put your hand just the way it was as you carried me to the grave. You know, Thomas, I wonder if this is you. Maybe you need to prove to me who you are?"

"If you touch me exactly as Thomas did I will know you. You must show me another thing. Where did the blood run down your side while you carried me to the grave. Only then will I know you are really who you say you are. Then if you are satisfied, Thomas, tell it to the world."

Thomas could only turn and hold Jesus legs and sob. "My brother, my Lord and my god!"

Jesus was quiet for a moment. The others began to see a smile slowly spreading across the resurrected face. His skin was still scarred from the beatings and the crown of thorns.

"Hey, brother, easy on the legs. They are still a little wobbly. Just be thankful this last three days has been an experience for me alone. You do not have to share the cross with me. One thing I must do by myself. Now it is complete. It is over and done now. Remember, my brother, I will always be with you."

# 68. Gray Chariot
## Acts 8:26-40; Psalm 22:25-31;
## 1 John 4:7-21 John 15:1-8
## Baptism after the Resurrection.
## Gospel Time: 600

El Zah stood easily in the cab of the Ethiopian government chariot. Going here, going there for the needs of the Ethiopian government was his total life. Usually, El Zah carried his traveling gear with him in his chariot. When El Zah came into a major city such as Jerusalem, he might be there a few days. Or, occasionally, he might be gone tomorrow.

In his earlier days, El Zah was bitter, torn between his own fate and the good life handed to him. His owner had money, respect and position among the nations around the Mediterranean Sea. His chariot carried the family seal of his owner and the Ethiopian mark inlaid on its armored sides. Everyone knew that family would take serious action if they molested the messenger for any reason.

El Zah had much of the best of life. He was a slave, but his owner trusted him with everything important to her. He traveled all over the area of northeast Africa, including the Nile River Valley of Egypt. He talked with heads of state from Syria to Libya. He prevented wars and worked to make life good for other Ethiopians trading or vacationing in the area.

Several times each year El Zah went home to Ethiopia. El Zah knew the importance of staying in touch with his own government. The discussions of the Ethiopian governmental councils and decision-makers were important to his own work. So whenever he could, El Zah traveled home to Ethiopia for new policy decisions and relationships.

In his official chariot, El Zah was a welcome addition to any caravan making the long trips. Traveling south and back north through the Nile Valley was always tricky. Traveling the road from Damascus to Alexandria, or to Morocco and return, was dangerous. A high-placed official, even of a foreign government, offered some protection from marauding thieves. They cared little about the family seals on the chariot. Yet this small defense worked both ways.

El Zah needed the protection of the caravans. Even a government official traveling alone had no protection from robbers or pirates. The official seal on his chariot carried little weight with highwaymen, especially outside Ethiopia. Few could read, and fewer cared what the inlays on the chariot might say, anyway. It was always best to be with an armed trading caravan. The caravan operator usually welcomed another strong arm and fast horse. An extra fighter might save lives or goods in case of attack.

As he traveled with a caravan, El Zah had lots of time to think about his own situation. His own parents gave him up to Queen Candace at his birth. They made him a eunuch in the belief this would deter him from any wishful thinking. He was not to worry about either his lineage, either past or future. In this way, he could and should focus on his Queen as his whole purpose in life. He should be happy just knowing he had no other responsibilities for life itself.

This only made El Zah more anxious about himself. The mutilation dis-connected him from generations who came before him. He would never have generations following him. None of the children he saw playing in the streets or fields along the Nile would know him. None would ever call him "Father" or "Grand-Dad." El Zah rode along the ancient highway to Addis Ababa. Even there, he could not contemplate warm hugs and kisses from a wife or children at home.

El Zah spent many bitter, lonely hours along that dusty road between Alexandria and Addis Ababa. As he grew into middle age, El Zah allowed this bitterness to overwhelm him. He was a highly successful man. Still he could not shake the impact on himself. Sometimes he could only see himself as an animal, a creature with no value.

Sometimes El Zah made little side trips into the Jewish communities of Israel, Egypt or Ethiopia as he traveled. His own parents were Jews, but El Zah knew nothing more about them. He did not even know much about Judaism as a religion or a society. He only knew it was his single tie with preceding or following generations.

On one of his first, El Zah made a point to travel the length of Israel, from Capernaum to Jerusalem. As he traveled, El Zah questioned many rabbis and elders about the faith. He learned about the great prophets of the north and the south, from Amos to Isaiah. He heard stories of the Great Exile, and saw the huge temple being rebuilt by the Herodians.

El Zah left Jerusalem to return again to Ethiopia. Now El Zah resolved to visit this promised land again whenever he could. After another journey to Libya and Morocco, he should be ready to return to the land of David and Josiah.

Meanwhile, he had work to do for his beloved Queen Candace. Acting as a chief statesman on her behalf call for his greatest skills. Publicly, he worked hard. Yet, at El Zah's darkest hours he turned to the ancient wise man, Isaiah.

Everyone in Israel and close by, from Damascus to Gaza, seemed to know something about this great seer and writer. Even small children could quote his poetry and promises to a traveling Ethiopian. It seemed everyone wanted to help El Zah understand their faith. Seen through the eyes of Isaiah, the great prophet of the south, it was a beautifully ethical faith. Some thoughtful rabbi gave him a tattered copy of a scroll of Isaiah for his own study.

After a few days in Jerusalem, El Zah again left Jerusalem for Addis Addiba. As he rode, his horses settled easily into the gait set by the few camels in the caravan. In a few moments, El Zah pulled out the scroll of Isaiah. He began to read the new words. He liked the words, but they confused him.

The new student of the old religion soon found himself struggling with almost every phrase of Isaiah. El Zah knew enough of the language that he could read the words. He had only a general sense of the meaning. The phrases and theology of Isaiah lost El Zah almost entirely. As he rode along the rough road in his chariot, El Zah talked to himself. He puzzled over the old language of his parents.

El Zah picked up a pattern in his travels which made his journeys more pleasant, and helped satisfy his curiosity. Often he picked up another traveler along the road. As they rode together, El Zah peppered the fellow traveler with questions. He wanted to know about geography, religion, politics, food, and anything else that came to mind. He came to know a lot about many people along the roads. He could speak several languages now, and even sing songs of people from all around the Mediterranean.

Now a young man appeared beside the chariot, half running, half walking. The man spoke words which El Zah recognized were a mixture of Aramaic and koine Greek. He asked by gestures if he could ride with the Ethiopian. With only a gesture and a smile between them, Philip stepped onto the platform of the chariot.

Philip tied his small roll to the chariot body. His eye caught a quick glimpse of the scroll of Isaiah in the hand of El Zah. Fascinated and excited now, Philip saw the Ethiopian's eyes beginning to scowl with misunderstanding and puzzle. He realized El Zah was trying to study the six-century old words of the great prophet of the Jews. Instantly, Philip recalled the gentle words in his ear. "Go over by that chariot. Stay close. You will have an opportunity to speak to him about me."

Now Philip knew he just had to speak. "Do you understand what you are reading there? Those are the words of Isaiah, the great prophet of the Jews."

El Zah could only answer from the heart. "I know these words. I know they tell about my life. I am just not sure what they say. How can I know what the words say? I have no one to explain them to me. I have no parents, and no children. I have not studied in school. A rabbi gave me this scroll, but I can only read the words. How can I know what they mean? What is he telling me with his words of life? My parents were Jews of Ethiopia, but I know almost nothing of their faith. Who will help me know the meaning of my own life?"

The questions momentarily stunned Philip. He expected to speak to this man about Jesus, but only after some persuasive argument. Yet an open invitation to lay it on the line came from a stranger. Of course, Philip made a monumental error. He assumed El Zah thought the words of Isaiah referred to Jesus, just crucified and resurrected in Jerusalem.

However, the Ethiopian could only see himself in the words of Isaiah. His years of lament over his own state of loneliness shaped his emotions. His separation from the generations of his own family tricked him. They invited him to see the world – and Isaiah's words – as centering on himself.

Philip talked about Jesus. He talked about Jesus being the focus of all of Judaism. He talked about Jesus being the central figure of all of history. Jesus especially was the central figure of the people of the Lord. His was the role of the core reality of the people of Moses. He also covered the people of David, the people of the Exile and the Return. Philip needed to talk about Jesus as the center of his own existence as a Greek and a Jew.

As Philip talked on, bouncing along in the Ethiopian government chariot, changes began to come to El Zah's heart. El Zah began to see changes in his own existence. He felt his personality, his nation, his inheritance now linked undeniably to the Judaism of this Philip. Well, and to Philip's leader, Jesus. He saw every part of himself attached to this man. Jesus became the center of the words, the life and the faith of Philip.

Slowly El Zah began to realize that his lack of lineage, family or generations did not matter any longer. He might be riding an Ethiopian chariot down a dusty Judaean road across the desert to Phoenicia. That was all right. Philip tied El Zah's heart through his own heart to a Galilean carpenter. Through that man, El Zah linked now to every man, woman and child on earth.

His horses plodded on along the dusty road now. As he rode, the Ethiopian tried to take in the meaning of this new and rewarding relationship. What a concept for him! Related and linked to every man, woman and child on the face of the earth! How could he seal this new status? How could he formally accept this new relationship through Jesus? How could he buy and lock himself into this new pattern of living and loving?

The small caravan began to stop for a mid-day rest alongside an oasis pool. Several caravans already paused there for noon rest, twenty or so miles southwest of Jerusalem. The day was not too hot, so the horses and camels could make good time. Most maintained about a steady three miles per hour. The road was pretty good, well constructed and maintained by the Romans. Now the pool of good water was really a gift. El Zah thought of the symbolism of the pool in his own life. He even began to see Philip as part of the Lord's gift to the wandering Ethiopian.

Suddenly, El Zah had a new notion, inspired by the presence of Philip and Jesus in his life. "Philip, I just now have a thought. What is to keep me from being baptized? That baptism will be the Lord's mark on me! With that mark, I will be a member of the family of the Lord! Even the Lord will know I am in the family of Jesus! I will be in your family, Philip! By the seals inlaid on the walls of this chariot people will know me. Everyone will know me also as a member of the family of Jesus. I will also be in the family of Peter, and John, and Mary, and all the rest! I need that very much. My baptism will reveal who I am. I will be a whole man. I will be free, just as you are! Let's do it, Philip. Here. Right now. In this pool!"

So the pool in the desert southwest of Jerusalem was the scene of a historic change. Philip baptized El Zah, a servant of Candace, queen of Ethiopia. Several travelers watched the little ritual. Traders, soldiers, diplomats, slaves, men, women. Camels and horses.

El Zah became family with every part of creation that day, lifted by the presence of the onlookers. Lifted by the Lord. Lifted by love.

Then El Zah climbed again into the gray chariot to continue his journey to Ethiopia. He looked around for his new brother to offer him a ride. More than mere hospitality, El Zah would learn so much from this man of faith. But, no. Philip was nowhere to be found.

Karl C Evans has served Jesus, the Church and the world community in many capacities and locations throughout his life. He has served as pastor of United Methodist, Presbyterian, and Evangelical Lutheran congregations in Idaho, Washington, Oregon, Georgia, Arizona and Nevada.

Karl has served various mission roles in the national church and in Arizona and Nevada. Karl has served multi-point parishes in Georgia and Oregon. He has established a new congregation in Oregon.

His education includes elementary and high school at Fruitland, Idaho; college at University of Puget Sound and Grays Harbor College. Degrees are from Willamette University (Salem, Oregon B.A. 1968), Emory University Candler School of Theology (Atlanta Georgia, 1970 M.Div) and Drew University (Madison New Jersey, 1985 D.Min.)

Karl and his wife, Donella, currently live in Oregon. Together they have four children, ten grandchildren and five great-grandchildren.

Karl's other books include: A Jubilee Workbook, CSS Publishing Co., 2009; Tales and Prayers for New Life in Christ, CSS Publishing Co.,2008; Gospel of Hope, Writer's Club, 2002; Stories That Heal, Drew University, 1985, And Crown Thy Good, Karl Evans, 1987.

Audio and presentation works now available include: A Jubilee Workshop, 2009; The Jesus Stories, 2010. Both are available from Karl Evans, karl4life@aol.com.

Made in the USA
San Bernardino, CA
09 October 2016